ENTERTAINMENT TECHNOLOGY PRESS

In taking advantage of the latest digital printing techniques, Entertainment Technology Press is approaching book publishing in a very different way. By establishing a wide range of highly specific technical books that can be kept up-to-date in a continuing publishing process, our plan is to cover the entertainment technology sector with a wide range of individual titles.

As will be seen by examining the back cover of this book, the ETP list is divided into various categories so as to allow sufficient room for generic growth and development of each title. To ensure the quality of the books and the success of the project the publishers are building up a team of authors who are practising in and well-respected by the industry. As specialists within a particular field of activity it is anticipated that each author will stay closely involved with 'their' title or titles for an extended period.

All Entertainment Technology Press titles have a dedicated area on the publisher's own website at www.etnow.com where latest information and up-dates can be accessed by purchasers of the books concerned. This additional service is included within the purchase price of all titles.

Readers and prospective authors are invited to submit any ideas and comments they may have on the Entertainment Technology Press series to the Series Editor either by post to the address below or by email to editor@etnow.com.

FOR REFERENCE ONLY

This title is sponsored by

BASICS

A BEGINNER'S GUIDE TO SPECIAL EFFECTS

Peter Coleman

Liverpool
Community
College

ENTERTAINMENT
TECHNOLOGY PRESS

Educational Series

BASICS
A BEGINNER'S GUIDE TO SPECIAL EFFECTS

Peter Coleman

Entertainment Technology Press

Basics
A Beginner's Guide to Special Effects

© Peter Coleman

First edition published September 2005 by
Entertainment Technology Press Ltd
The Studio, High Green, Great Shelford, Cambridge CB2 5EG
Internet: www.etnow.com

ISBN 1 904031 33 1

A title within the
Entertainment Technology Press Educational Series
Series editor: John Offord

CODE / BFX001

CONTENTS

ACKNOWLEDGEMENTS

With thanks to:

Jo Beaumont-Ward and Mike Savage (Health & Safety Officer at Stage
   Electrics)
My proof-readers, who have kept me on the straight and narrow path.
And all at Stage Electrics who have given me encouragement and support.

INTRODUCTION

For anyone not familiar with *Basics – A Beginner's Guide to Stage Lighting* and *Basics – A Beginners Guide to Stage Sound,* I should explain straight away that the aim of this book is to provide a (hopefully) simple explanation of the topic listed. It is not intended to be a complete reference work, in this case for things involved in the broad description of 'special effects' and, as has been the case with previous *Basics* publications, you are likely to find that a fair amount of time is spent dealing with things which you probably didn't expect to be involved with when producing your 'special effects'.

Over the years and while working in virtually every form of theatre and the performing arts, I have seen, been involved with and, quite often, been asked to produce many different forms of special effect. In straight plays, pantomimes, revues, ballet, musicals, grand opera, fashion shows and commercial product launches, there always seems to be a need for something out of the ordinary.

Many of these special effects are indeed very special, so much so that they won't get much of a mention in this book. That's partly because they involve very high cost, but also because they are way above the ability, *or the requirements,* of the average user: i.e. to literally blow up a complete stage set full of giant statues – something like a cross between Stonehenge and the Easter Island monoliths – by mimicking a gunpowder trail laid onto the floor by one of the cast. This sort of film set effect, which we are all used to seeing at the cinema is rather difficult to produce as a regular event live on stage every night!

No, that sort of thing is beyond the scope of *Basics,* but don't worry, there's plenty left for those of you who want a special effect that's on the sensible side of normal.

In previous *Basics* books I have given them one or more alternative titles. You might think there isn't much of an alternative title to *A Beginner's Guide to Special Effects,* but how about *Some Basics in Health and Safety Planning,* or perhaps, *The Risk Assessment – the Starting Point for Special Effects.* At least these two alternatives should give you some idea of what's in store for you in the following pages.

I should also point out that my background in this area comes from working in and latterly supplying the needs of, theatrical performances, where of course many of these effects have to work in real time (live) and in close proximity to the performers and audience.

PROLOGUE

I think one thing we would all agree on is that as with most things in the modern technological age, the nature and impact of the theatrical effects that we can create, are now bigger, better, simpler, and hopefully safer, than we have ever had access to before. However – and it's a rather *big* however – some of the effects that you will want to use will bring you into contact, although not necessarily in conflict, with Health and Safety legislation. Therefore, in the planning of your event and the use of special effects you will almost certainly need to take this factor into account.

So just what constitutes these so called 'special effects'? It's a question that's very difficult to answer directly. For instance, the use of a pyrotechnic flash or an explosive maroon is pretty obvious, but how would you categorise the flying of a member of the acting company – as required in Peter Pan for example? What about the use of smoke? A falling snow effect? A bottle smashed over someone's head? The projected image of moving clouds? The list is almost endless and yes, they are all 'effects' – and by not being exactly ordinary, they must also by definition be 'special'.

Something that's often overlooked in the planning and use of an effect is whether it will need a dedicated operator. For reasons which at first may not be obvious, many effects do, and this very fact leads us straight into the issues of Health and Safety legislation.

Leaving aside specific effects for a moment, just pause to consider the wider implications of the Health and Safety at Work Act 1974. The basis of the Act, and no I'm not going to start quoting great chunks of it, is that it applies to every place of work, and while you might not have realised it, that means it will apply to the venue you are going to be using. It does not matter whether it's a school hall, church, or theatre. Small or large, amateur or professional, a local authority-controlled town hall or a tiny village hall – they will all be subject to this legislation.

The tasks to be undertaken within a place of work, especially where there could be an element of risk or hazard, are required to be identified. This identification is known as a 'risk assessment', and is a written statement including, where necessary, statements about the prescribed methods of operation. This could be for the operation of some sort of manufacturing machinery – perhaps an overhead crane, a fork lift truck in a factory environment and of course, in many cases in your performance space, your special effect.

Now we have to apply a degree of common sense at this point, because not all of your special effects are going to warrant a form of risk assessment. For example, a gobo in a lantern projecting the image of snowflakes is no more than the use of a lantern within your existing pool of equipment, but a pyrotechnic effect which uses a small explosive charge – well that's obviously in a different category.

I'm sure you can see where this is leading: you produce a risk assessment, for example for the pyrotechnic flash, a part of which will have to make reference to a dedicated control device (detonator), and of course someone tasked to operate it. So a part of your planning for certain types of special effect will need an understanding on your part that dedicated personnel are sometimes needed.

As we work our way through the various special effects on offer, I will indicate the sort of risk assessment involved. This is in the form of a simple check box sheet (see facing page). It is by no means the industry standard, if there is such a thing, but it will give you the basic information you need. The mere fact that you can show an understanding of the requirement for this assessment shows that you have at least some understanding of Health and Safety legislation.

'Here we go again' – I can hear a few dissenting voices out there making the usual comment about a little knowledge being a dangerous thing. To make myself clear, I am not trying to provide a full description of Health and Safety legislation, or the 1974 Act, so please don't run off with the idea that to follow my notes and make your own risk assessments will make it all right. What I must say is that much compliance with Health and Safety legislation does put the onus of 'safe use' onto the individual. The difficult part is knowing, or at least making an assessment, of just where you have to stop and take more experienced advice. Perhaps the answer to this is within the detail of your risk assessment, for you might argue that if the risk is likely to cause serious injury, or even death, then you might need a little more help in making your assessment! At this point I would return you to the beginning of this paragraph.

One thing that I suggest you don't lose sight of in making a risk assessment is that at the end of the process your best, possibly even your only assessment, is simply not to do it. Of course, that is likely to bring you into conflict with those people who asked you to produce the effect in the first place and some of them might regard this is a bit of a cop-out, but I suggest this is not so. Remember the reason for all this planning and assessment is to try to stay

RISK ASSESSMENT

Area	Stage & Auditorium
Activity	Rig & Focus of Performance Lighting

Risk Assessment Date ....

No. of Persons	T/Leaders Managers	Operatives 1	2	Trainees 0	Casuals 0	Others

Hazard	Means of Access (*)	Authorised to work	Suitably Trained	Equipment PAT in date	All Personnel	Selected Personnel	Exposure Rating	Probability Rating	Severity Rating	Risk Rating
Working at Height	✓	✓	✓	✓		✓	Frequent	Frequent	A&E	Acceptable
Working in poorly lit areas		✓	✓	✓	✓		Frequent	Frequent	1st Aid	Acceptable
Working with class 1 portable appliances		✓	✓	✓		✓	Frequent	Frequent	1st Aid	Acceptable
Working on raked stage floor		✓	✓			✓	Continuous	Continuous	1st Aid	Acceptable
Working in confined spaces		✓	✓				Occasional	Remote	A&E	Acceptable
Slips Trips & Falls					✓		Continuous	Continuous	1st Aid	Acceptable
Manual Handling (lifting)		✓	✓		✓		Frequent	Occasional	A&E	Acceptable
Falling Objects					✓		Occasional	Occasional	A&E	Acceptable
Young Person under 16 present	✗	✗	✗	✗	✗	✗	N/A	N/A	N/A	N/A
Other working practices taking place	✗	✗	✗	✗	✗	✗	N/A	N/A	N/A	N/A

ADDITIONAL CONTROLS:

1. (*) Means of Access IS PROVIDED
2. Correct Lifting Technique Training IS PROVIDED
3. PPE (Gloves) IS PROVIDED
4. PPE (Hard Hats) for Floor Workers IS PROVIDED
5. No other personnel present during focus works

Signature

Name

Position

CONCLUSION :

ACCEPTABLE	✓ or X
ACCEPTABLE (with additional controls)	✓ or X [✓]
NOT ACCEPTABLE	✓ or X

safe. Just consider the likely outcome if you to proceed with an action containing some risk, were it to cause an accident. You could expect that having been subject to a form of risk assessment which had a negative end result, that if the action was then carried out and an injury were to result, the Health and Safety executive who may investigate would be likely to take the named individual – that's you – to task and to court. You could face a charge of a breach of some form of regulation, all made indefensible by the fact that the risk assessment had shown a problem in the first place. Remember accidents can happen but the risk assessment will play a major part in making you and others aware of the risks involved, and sometimes the assessment is not to take the risk despite the needs and prompting of others.

For those of you who really want to get to grips with Heath and Safety legislation, I offer the following, as some none-too-light bedtime reading:

- The Health and Safety at Work Act 1974 and as amended.
- The British Pyrotechnists Association & Explosive Industry Group *Firework Handbook.*
- The ABTT code of practice for the theatre industry *Pyrotechnics & Smoke Effects*

For anyone who is now confused by all this talk about Health and Safety and Risk Assessments, let me offer a couple of examples:

1. An amateur group putting on a pantomime production has a need for a pyrotechnic flash effect, to cover the entrance of the good fairy or the demon king. They make a risk assessment in line with the requirements of the village hall where they are performing, taking due regard to the proximity of the acting company, the set, costumes and properties in use, and any existing fire or other local authority regulations covering a stage performance.

Their decision is to proceed with the planned effect, there being an identified risk that can be offset or covered by having a person dedicated to be in control of the effect, coupled with a detailed briefing to all members of the performing company and technical staff.

2. A junior and infant school putting on a pantomime production have a need for a pyrotechnic flash effect to cover the entrance of the good fairy or the demon king. They make a risk assessment in line with the requirements of the school hall where they are performing, taking due regard to the proximity of the acting company, the set, costumes and properties in use and any existing fire or other local authority regulations covering a stage performance.

Their decision is *not* to proceed with the planned effect, there being an identified risk that, despite instructions, there would be a high probability of young children standing too close to the effect.

From this you can see that the same effect has to be assessed depending upon the circumstances of its use.

As I said in the introduction, your thoughts about making a special effect probably didn't include all this talk of health and safety or risk assessments. But in today's world, certainly in the UK, this is all very real. To the layperson it all might seem way over the top – yet another instance of the 'nanny state' getting in the way of people enjoying a harmless pastime. I'm sorry, but if that's how you feel about it, I suggest you are taking a somewhat out of date view of life. The legislation surrounding health and safety has been with us for many years (*Health and Safety at Work Act 1974*) and the really bad news is that ignorance of the law provides no defence.

It might help you to understand in my *basic* terms just how the law regarding health and safety works. It's not much different from what you would expect English law to be. The Health and Safety Executive – the governing body that forms and enforces Health and Safety law – is a little like a policeman, in that it will act when it sees a breach of Health and Safety regulations. This is usually as the result of an investigation by them following an accident. *Remember that it is an accident in a place of work, not your private dwelling house, and generally not on the roads.* From the investigation it will decide whether or not to bring any prosecution, but here's where it's a little different from most other law enforcing agencies, for it will only bring a prosecution if it is certain the case is proven. You could take the view that at this point the only reason for any action at law is to simply find out how big the fine will be, or in extreme cases how long the custodial sentence will be. That may well be, but the real point I'm trying to make for your information is that what you do in a place of work really has to take account of whatever Health and Safety legislation is applicable in that workplace, otherwise the penalties can be severe.

So far in matters Health and Safety, I have been pointing deliberately at the pyrotechnic effect. It's rather obvious really – letting off small controlled explosive devices, indoors and fairly close to people, is bound to carry some element of risk. But don't think that it's only the pyrotechnic effect that has a risk attached to it – far from it. I mentioned a little earlier about flying members of the acting company. I suggest that this is not something to try, unless after proper training and with the correct equipment. There are lots of things that are seen on the performance stage and sometimes on television, which are mistaken as an easy effect to reproduce. Sadly, this is mostly not the case and when coupled with a flawed mindset of a person whose desired artistic need is actually miles away from reality, serious problems are just waiting to happen.

I will cite one of my favourite cases. Way back in the 1980s, in the era of the first Star Wars films, a lady came into the trade counter of a theatrical supplier, asking if she could buy full sheets of colour filter – that's about 4ft x 2ft. This was not a particularly unusual request until she told us what she needed them for. We were quite shocked, but probably not as shocked as her acting company would have been. Some enterprising soul had made her up a couple of the Star Wars light sabres, using 4ft fluorescent tubes. Goodness knows what sort of electrical jiggery-pokery had been used and how the combatants were ever supposed to fight a mock battle, being tethered to a mains cable just didn't seem to matter. We pointed out, as politely as we could, that apart from the things actually smashing on a regular basis, the whole idea was ludicrously dangerous. The lady was crestfallen; she was quite convinced that that's how it was done on the film!

So you see, not everything in the world of special effects is quite what it may seem. Or perhaps I had it wrong all these years, and maybe they really did use fluorescent tubes!

1 PYROTECHNICS

Pyrotechnics (from the Greek)
Pyro: resulting from or by the action of fire of heat; Tekhnikos: of art or skill.

A pyrotechnic is the obvious 'effect' and probably the one that's likely to cause the most concern. After all, it's an explosive device – an indoor firework. Over many years I have lost count of the times I have been asked for advice about how and where to use a particular pyrotechnic effect, and my usual advice is quite simple: "If you are unsure about using any form of pyrotechnic effect, then don't."

This being a *Basics* book, I am only going to deal with a few of the best known and most widely used pyrotechnic effects, and within this range of effects I am going to promote the use of the pre-loaded cartridge system.

There are a number of companies who, in recent years, have used this type of system – generally making this area of 'effects' much safer and better for us all. I make no apologies for making reference to one of the best known of these companies – LeMaitre Ltd – who have become one of the largest manufacturers and supplier of this type of product, with their 'industry standard' theatrical pyrotechnic effects.

Alongside the actual effects has come a safe and simple firing system which, when used in accordance with the manufacturer's instructions, provides the user with if not a completely fool-proof means of setting off the chosen effect, then certainly something 95% better than what went before.

All that may sound as if I'm taking manufacturers to task for not getting it 100% right, but that's not my intention. After all, no one generally blames any of the car manufacturers for road accidents. The point is that it's you – the user – that has the ultimate responsibility for the safe use of what can be a dangerous effect.

And I don't want to be seen to be against the use of the pyrotechnic effect. In the right place, used in a safe and correct way, they are fabulous – and nothing else will do the job. They will enhance your production, but you really must be sure that your production and the venue can handle the consequences of the effect. As in the scenario detailed earlier, it may be that you simply cannot make safe use of the effect because of personnel in close proximity to it – but that's not the only consideration.

You will need to consider a number of other factors, when looking at the risk assessment, such as smoke detectors, smoke logging, storage and transport. Obviously some of this goes past the point of 'safe use' at the instant of the effect. Taking the last two issues first, how are you going to store and keep safe the pyrotechnics to be used? And how are you going to transport them to your venue? At face value you could regard your effect as no more than the use of fireworks for your November 5th celebrations, except for the fact that you are going to be using them within a place of work. So certainly where storage is concerned, both you the user and those responsible for the venue, will need to agree a suitable secure storage facility.

Regarding transportation, try contacting your motor insurance company and ask them for special cover for the transportation of these goods. I'll save you the bother: more than 50% and probably as many as 90% of companies simply won't give you any cover, and those that do will make you pay a large premium. Yes, I know it's only one or two journeys once or twice a year, but these things are explosive devices that carry an EN *(European Normal)* or BS *(British Standard)* classification, when being moved in quantity. So be prepared for additional expense in the matter of transportation.

So the pyrotechnics are safely delivered to your venue and stored away, but you are still left with those other issues I mentioned. Having got the effect out of the way safely, you are left with the aftermath of it. Of course this is all part of the planning, but it's surprising how many people just ignore or forget this part of the effect. All of the flashes, bangs and smoke effects will often set off smoke detectors and quite often in large modern buildings, these smoke detectors are linked to the fire alarm system with an automated dial-up to the local fire station.

Do you have any idea how much your local fire authority charge for a false alarm call out? Well, it probably varies across the country, but get ready for a bill of several hundred pounds! And for anyone silly enough to disable or interfere with a smoke alarm detector, the consequences are equally severe and rightly so. Yes, I know that you have seen many such effects used without any problems in theatres and other such venues, where there are smoke detectors. That's probably because the venue, realising a need for the use of such effects, has had the foresight and planning to have their alarm system set up in zones, so that for 'performance works', a selected zone may be disabled. This is of course all done with the risk-assessed blessings of the buildings operating procedures – all written down carefully and strictly adhered to.

Take account of smoke logging – simply too much smoke in your building. For the single or occasional effect, you shouldn't have a problem, but there are a few productions, for example Gilbert and Sullivan's *The Sorcerer*, in which if you were to follow the text, there is excessive use of the flash effect. I know of one production of this piece where the build up of smoke was so great that by the end of the first scene, the performers couldn't see each other across the stage, let alone the seated audience! Most manufacturers of pyrotechnic effects offer a wide and varied range which is likely to include a small, medium and large size of the desired effect, so you should be able to use the size best suited to your venue, in both the actual effect and its smoke output.

I made comment about promoting the use of the pre-loaded, cartridge type effect. This type of device now accounts for about 98% of the basic pyrotechnic effects used in theatrical performance. It has a number of major plus points over the old system of loose magnesium powder being set off by blowing a piece of low value fuse wire.

1   In the modern cartridge system the user is not exposed to any of the explosive charge. It is all kept sealed away inside the cartridge by a lightweight paper top cover, which is destroyed at the instant of detonation.

2   The amount of charge or powder used is consistent, dependent upon the size of the cartridge selected: small, medium or large; therefore the ability to overcharge the device is removed.

3   The cartridge holder (flash box) and firing mechanism (detonator) and the cables that link them together are designed for that purpose. Modern versions even carry a *cartridge present* indicator to give added information to the user.

4   The success rate of the pre-loaded cartridge is many times higher than found in the old systems.

5   You will find that most local authority controlled venues, coming under the control of a local fire authority fire officer, will be aware of the cartridge type system and generally accept its use. The same cannot be said of a home made detonating system and loose unspecified quantities of magnesium flash powder.

The cartridge has two small pins on the bottom, which locate and provide connection into the flash pod. The loaded pod then connects to the detonator with low value twin flex terminated in small dedicated connectors.

The detonator in its simple form is either a two or six channel unit and will connect to the main power supply. An integral transformer provides the low voltage necessary to

Le Maitre Pyroflash detonator, pod and assorted cartridges.

fire the cartridge. Once the chosen loaded flash pod has been connected to the selected channel of the detonator, a selection switch brings it under the control of the firing button. There is a key switch provided with which the user arms the detonator. This provides the final security checkpoint in firing the effect. I suggest that for the vast majority of users it is unwise to attempt to build your own detonator.

The important and critical factor in setting off the pyrotechnic effect is in two parts and both are relevant to the person in control of it. Firstly the operator must have a clear line of sight to the effect and the operation of the detonator must be under their manual control – not remotely fired by some other electrical circuit such as a cue from the lighting control desk.

Secondly, it is the sole discretion of the operator as to whether or not the effect is fired, depending upon actual site conditions and not just because the cue has been called by the stage management running the production.

For the basic flash or instant smoke effect, you will be required to purchase the cartridges in boxed quantities of 12. Your retailer cannot sell the cartridges singly, as to comply with the law and regulations governing the sale of these items, they have to be sold in the packaging from the manufacturers which contain instructions for use and a means of safe transportation.

The most commonly used cartridge effect is the standard theatrical (magnesium) flash cartridge, available in small, medium and large sizes. To clarify this, the size reference is relating to the load of the cartridge, not the actual size, which is the same for all within a specific description.

Now we need to go back to some of that Health and Safety legislation paperwork again. A part of the legislation is called COSHH (*Control Of Substances Hazardous to Health*) and in the workplace – your factory floor, office block, supermarket and of course your performance venue – there will be a COSHH register. If you didn't know it before, you should know that it is the law for every place of work to carry such a register and every substance that you can buy, use and store in the venue will have (sorry, *should* have) a COSHH data sheet kept in your register. This will spell out the details of what the substance is, how it reacts in specific conditions, and what effects it will have when in contact with you or me. In short, it's the technical data sheet for whatever substance is involved, and all manufacturers are duty bound by law to produce this information. In the case of the pyrotechnic device, each different effect type will have a data sheet such as the ones on the following pages.

The information contained within the product data sheet is all part of your risk assessment. In the case of the flash cartridge, it will give information relevant to the assessment, all of which enforces your case that you actually know something about the product you are using to create the effect.

The final piece of information I offer in connection with all things Health and Safety related may provide some solace to those of you who had just about given up, thinking it was all too much trouble. There is an often-used phrase that says: "shall have taken all reasonable steps to prevent danger". The precise interpretation of this is rather broad as it could be taken as meaning: "I've read the instructions and have made sure that the pyrotechnic effect to be used is sited and detonated correctly". However, if one of your acting company by accident stands too close to the effect and is burned as a consequence, you the operator could still be found negligent for setting it off. I hope you can see just how complex the issue of Health and Safety can be in the workplace (which is your performance space).

This whole section, aimed at the pyrotechnic effect, has obviously been rather highjacked by the Health and Safety issues raised. I can't apologise for this – it's a matter of fact that it is a very important issue and one which you should not – indeed must not – ignore. But before we get too side-tracked, I will try to cover just a few of the other basic things about the pyrotechnic effect.

I have made reference to the cartridge system; indeed I have even described the cartridge and the flash pod that you plug it into. But you will find that even within one specific manufacturer's product range, there are two different types

Material Safety Data Sheet

The following information has been prepared in accordance with the Health and Safety at work act and the Control of Substances Hazardous to Health regulations. Users should always consult the current legislation prior to any intended use.

Product:	Theatrical Flash; Small, Medium and Large	**IMDG Packing:**	P135
U.N. Hazard Division:	1.4	**IMDG EmS CODE:**	1-04
Compatibility Group:	S	**IMDG Stowage Cat.**	05
UN Serial No.:	0432	**IATA:**	135
P.S.N:	ARTICLES PYROTECHNIC for technical purposes.	**ADR:**	EP35

This device has been approved by the Health and Safety Executive. Certificate Serial No.72-Z-00397, Schedule 1.

DESCRIPTION of PRODUCT and EFFECT

A squat black plastic cylindrical cartridge (Ø52 x 22mm) with a paper cap at the top and two metal contact pins protruding from the base.

On ignition this device produces a bright flash and a puff of smoke. The flash from this device produces radiant heat, which should be taken into consideration when positioning this device.

Size	Ave. Noise level at 4m indoors / dB
Small	90.6
Medium	98.6
Large	102.5

USER INSTRUCTIONS

INTENDED FOR PROFESSIONAL USE ONLY BY PERSONS OVER 18 YEARS OF AGE.

This effect must only be used in conjunction with a Le Maitre Pyroflash firing system and holders No liability of any sort will be entertained by Le Maitre where their pyrotechnics are used with an unapproved firing system. The instructions for the Le Maitre firing system must be observed at all times.

It is essential that a risk assessment be carried out prior to the use of any pyrotechnic effect, taking into consideration the location of the members of the audience, crew and performers with respect to the effect produced by the device when in the firing location.

ENSURE that all pyrotechnic devices can be observed before and during firing in order that nothing has changed with regards to the location i.e. personnel too close, scenery moved etc. DO NOT FIRE if any personnel become too close to the device.

It is recommended that tests be carried out without any personnel present in a totally safe environment, to ensure that the effect produced is that required. Where decibel levels are indicated it is advised that readings can change according to environmental conditions and it is essential that operators bear this in mind when using these devices. If the operator is unsure as to the nature of the effect produced by a device then we recommend that the device be tested out of doors first, employing all relevant safety equipment including ear defenders and safety glasses.

DO NOT SMOKE at any time when dealing with pyrotechnic devices.

Example of product data sheet.

IN THE EVENT OF A MIS-FIRE / DISPOSAL INSTRUCTIONS: If the device fails to fire, isolate the effect from the firing system. Check that the circuit has been connected correctly and repeat the firing sequence. If unsuccessful disconnect the firing circuit again, remove the device from its firing position and return to its original packaging to await disposal.

Disposal: Submerge in a large bucket of water and gently pierce the paper membrane to allow the water to enter the device. Leave soaking outside in a secure area for a minimum of 48 hours then dispose of in accordance with local regulations.

FORMULATION AND PHYSICAL APPEARANCE OF EXPLOSIVE: (refers to un-fired device)
This device contains: This device contains: A free flowing grey powder comprising potassium perchlorate, potassium nitrate magnesium and aluminium powders.

EXPOSURE LIMITS: (refers to composition before firing)

8-hour TWA total inhalable dust. 10 mg / cubic metre
8-hour TWA total respirable dust. 4 mg / cubic metre

INHALATION OF SMOKE PRODUCED FROM THE EFFECT SHOULD BE AVOIDED. EXCESSIVE SMOKE INHALATION MAY CAUSE RESPIRATORY IRRITATION, DIFFICULTY IN BREATHING, HEADACHES, NAUSEA AND MAY RESULT IN VOMITING. IN NORMAL USE WITH ADEQUATE VENTILATION THE SMOKE PRODUCED SHOULD NOT BE A PROBLEM. HOWEVER ANY PERSON FOUND TO BE SUFFERING FROM SMOKE INHALATION SHOULD BE REMOVED TO FRESH AIR AND MEDICAL ASSISTANCE SOUGHT.

STORAGE CONDITIONS: Store in a cool dry place, humidity should preferably be less than 70%. Avoid extreme temperatures. In particular sub-zero temperatures where freezing and re-thaw can alter the performance of the article.

A local Authority permit may be required for storage in bulk. The local Trading Standards Department should be consulted for further details.

EMERGENCY PROCEEDURES

SPILLAGE: Sweep up any loose powder and packaging and dispose of by following the disposal instructions. Avoid skin contact. In case of contact with skin wash hands immediately.

FIRE: Cool Pyrotechnic devices and / or packages with water and remove them if possible.

NOTE:

1. The information given in this sheet is for the guidance of Le Maitre Customers and should be checked against current standards and limits published by the H.S.E.

2. The Information given here is true and reliable to the best of our knowledge.

3. The company cannot be responsible for any loss or damage through any miss-use of the product.

4. Smoke, however little may cause problems for asthma sufferers.

EMERGENCY INFORMATION

SALES:	Le Maitre Ltd	FACTORY	Le Maitre Ltd.
	6 Forval Close, Wandle Way,		Fourth Drove, Fengate,
	Mitcham, Surrey.		Peterborough
	CR4 4NE		PE1 5UR
	Tel: +44 (0) 208 646 2222		Tel: +44 (0) 1733 346 824
	Fax: +44 (0) 208 646 1955		Fax: +44 (0) 1733 568619

Example of product data sheet.

of flash pod, and the connecting pin hole centres are different so you cannot plug any cartridge into any box. They are designed that way on purpose, and here's why.

The standard range of products, which includes most of the flashes and instant smoke effects, fits into the standard pod and is designed to discharge the effect straight upwards. There are a number of cartridge loaded effects which discharge a paper based product, such as confetti or streamers. These cartridges are often required to fire at an angle and not simply straight up, so for them there is a special angled pod which, as the name implies, allows you to achieve this. However because it may be deemed dangerous to fire one of the instant effect cartridges at an angle,

Le Maitre angled pod loaded with large streamer cartridge.

the two pod types have different pin centres, so that when used correctly you will only be able to fire the instant cartridge at the correct (straight up) angle and as a consequence of this arrangement, it follows that the cartridges have the locating pins set to suit the correct pod.

We are getting close to the end of the *basic* information, which looks as if it's all designed to put you off using any sort of pyrotechnic effect at all. Remember one of the very first comments I made: "If you are unsure about using any form of pyrotechnic effect, then don't". Well, of course I know very many of you will go ahead, some even as first-time users, so especially for you please don't regard all my warnings in the wrong way. I'm not trying to stop you; I'm just trying to make you aware of what's involved in keeping pace with today's legislation and to keep you and those around you safe.

So now at last let me list just a few of the basic effects on offer and a very brief description of what they do.

Theatrical Flash
An instant bright white flash, followed instantly by a rising mushroom of white smoke. Available in small, medium, large size and loud report (loud report is very loud).

Red, Amber and Green Flash
An instant bright coloured flash, followed immediately by a rising mushroom

of white smoke. It is available in a medium size only. If you want to have the whole flash effect coloured including the smoke, then position a lantern directly above it and plot a lighting cue to bring on the lantern as the effect is fired, with a follow-on cue to remove it. That way you can make the smoke whatever colour you want.

Silver Star Cartridge
Very similar to the Theatrical Flash, but the instant bright flash has the addition of silver sparks. It is available in small, medium, large size.

Coloured Smoke: 6-8 second duration (a range of colours is available). From the instant of firing, which produces a very small low volume report, the smoke will issue from the cartridge for 6-8 seconds. Caution: the smoke contains a dye which will stain clothes, scenery, curtains, etc if in too close proximity.

White Smoke Pellets (only available in white)
A small (12mm x 12mm) pellet which, when lit with a naked flame, will issue smoke for 25 -30 seconds burning without flame and leaving an ash residue. Should be used on a non-flammable base. The pellets have a strong acrid odour.

There are many other cartridge type effects and of these many derivatives your retailer, or LeMaitre Ltd will be able to give you details of just what is available.

Now just in case you thought you had finished with the flashes and bangs of pyrotechnics, I have to disappoint you as we have hardly scratched the surface. All I've talked about so far are just a few cartridge based effects, and a lot of health and safety issues. There are loads more effects, so let's look at a few that need special attention.

Maroons
Maroons simply provide a loud bang and are not designed for the visual impact. They are usually detonated somewhere backstage, but close enough to have the desired effect on the audience. Again these will be available in small, medium and large sizes, but unlike the cartridge type effects maroons don't just plug into a firing pod, they come with a short flex (pair of wires) attached and it's up the user to apply a voltage.

Le Maitre Maroon.

Anything from 9v up to a mains 230v supply, will set them off. It's quite common to find the same firing detonator unit used for the cartridges used to set off a maroon. All that's needed is a short converter cable (known as a maroon jumper) to provide the ability to connect the cable to the maroon.

All maroons should be used within a designated metal enclosure, known as a 'bomb tank'. It is made of a heavy gauge metal and most importantly has a lid or top made from some form of heavy gauge wire mesh. This allows the force of the explosion to be safely vented upwards, the mesh top ensuring that the majority of any case fragments of the maroon are kept inside the tank. The modern bomb tank will normally be built in a style providing multiple compartments, one for each maroon used. This becomes vitally important when using multiple maroon effects, because you will find that if you place several maroons in the same single compartment tank, the action of the first one or two maroons will tend to blow the wire connections off the others, so you will reach a point where your intended maroons just won't fire.

For regular users, you may have your own bomb tank made up, or you can buy a purpose-made one. Some occasional users will use a metal dustbin with layers of wire mesh securely fixed on top. Whatever the choice, two things are critical:

1 The location of the bomb tank: you must make sure that everyone likely to be in the vicinity of it knows about it, and before firing check to make sure that no one is standing too close to it.

2 The second factor may seem rather obvious but you must make sure that nothing has been left on top of the tank because the explosion created will send even quite heavy objects into the air!

All maroons look quite small and insignificant, but the explosive force that they generate shows that they are anything but. All explosions are made more violent when enclosed, and in the case of the maroon, unlike the cartridge effects which have a paper top cover, a maroon is an explosive charge that is totally enclosed in a hard shell casing. So, for the fist-time user, how are you to know what size of maroon to use? Well, a lot depends upon the size of the venue you are performing in, but the following may help. Taking the LeMaitre maroon range as a guide:

small maroon = starting pistol (loud crack)
medium maroon = shot gun (in close proximity)
large maroon = two shotguns (twice the medium maroon)

These examples are very general and a lot will depend upon the venue and the location of the bomb tank in relation to the audience.

Confetti Cannon

There is one effect which uses a medium maroon as a part of it: the 'confetti cannon'. For those who have not seen or experienced one, this is a metal cylinder about 12" diameter and 18" high, which is loaded with confetti or other paper or lightweight product that sits on top of a cardboard base, below which sits a maroon set inside a small metal receptacle. When

Confetti Cannon.

detonated, the displacement of air caused by the explosion pushes the cardboard and the confetti up and out of the cylinder. It's a great effect in the right place and usually the biggest problem with it is to find someone to clean up the mess afterwards! And it's here that you just might find the makings of a problem.

You can buy the confetti, in 1kg bags, and even pay a little extra for the fire retardant treated type, and of course this is a consumable item. For a one-off event that's all very well, but when the effect is used in a production with many performances, there is a tendency for users to sweep up and re-use the confetti. Now beware! In sweeping up you will inevitably collect a few things that you really don't want in your confetti cannon, such as drawing pins, paperclips and even small stones – in fact any small hard object, which will become a high velocity projectile when you fire the cannon the next time.

Microdets

There are some very small maroons and in the LeMaitre range these are called 'Microdets'. They offer a much lower intensity effect than seen in the standard maroons. They are used to simulate bullet strikes or small explosive faults in machinery or electronic components and

Le Maitre Microdet.

are more often found in the film and TV industry special effects departments, but they sometimes find their way into theatrical productions. In themselves their use is probably beyond the *basics* of this book but my reason for making mention of them here is because there is a very special effect that uses them, and I really want to stress that you should not get involved with it! That's the bullet hits and associated blood bags, worn by performers. This is a very specialist job and I believe should not be attempted by anyone who is not specifically trained for it. Indeed I believe that all of the larger manufacturers of pyrotechnics will have some products which they will only supply to specified users, such as the military, police and fire authorities, for training and simulation purposes.

In the UK there are four categories of fireworks, as covered in BS 7114, 1989 and the first, category 1, is for indoor fireworks. The remaining categories cover outdoor event and display fireworks. There have been some attempts by government to help to ensure safety standards, in the general supply and operation of fireworks for public use. The 1997 Firework (Safety) Regulations have been introduced, but unfortunately there is still no specific legislation or law that deals with theatrical pyrotechnics. As far as the law is concerned, if you are over 18 years of age, it all comes under the same category as buying fireworks for a bonfire night party. In other parts of the world, such as Canada and the USA for instance, there are quite strict regulations governing people trained and permitted to operate theatrical pyrotechnics, but for use in the UK you are not required to undertake any specific training.

My personal view is that this is wrong, mainly because over the years I have seen the consequences of getting it wrong, which has often resulted in visits to the casualty department of the local hospital.

So, finally, where pyrotechnics are concerned, beware and be careful.

2 SMOKE AND DRY ICE

There will be a number of reasons why you may need smoke in your production: the need for a smoke effect simulating fire or an explosion is fairly obvious. However, you may not want to use smoke for this reason, but simply to create a smoke filled atmosphere. There's nothing like smoke to accentuate the lighting for certain types of performance, but how this is delivered and arrives on stage needs some careful consideration. Remember my comments about smoke-logging the space when using pyrotechnics? Well you can do the same thing with the overuse of a smoke machine. However, since the output is controllable, this shouldn't be a problem.

If you are looking for the atmosphere effect, then you probably don't need a smoke machine at all, but a 'haze' machine. It is something very similar, but uses a different type of fluid and has a low level constant output.

However, the smoke we are dealing with in this section is that generated by a smoke machine. There are a host of manufacturers offering machines that will produce smoke and in the main they all do the same job, so let's get one or two generic things out of the way at the outset.

1 All smoke machines output white smoke only.
2 All smoke produced is non-carcinogenic.
3 All smoke will activate smoke detectors.
4 All smoke machines have to heat up before they are ready to use.

So, from the many varied shapes, sizes and models available, how do you know which one to use? How do they differ? Generally in terms of output they will fall into two categories: high or low output. The low output machines may be classified as the standard models, whilst the high output machines offer both high volume and a higher instant output and are generally used in larger venues or where a dramatic or large instant volume is required.

Almost all smoke machines need a mains power supply (although there are

A typical smoke machine with fluid bottle.

one or two very small battery operated ones) in order to power the heat exchange unit and the pump needed to move the smoke fluid through the heat exchanger. The consequence of needing a mains power supply usually means that the machine is not exactly portable, so when in use the smoke is likely to emanate from just one location. You will find that most smoke machines are relatively small and if necessary can be hidden within parts of the set or scenery.

Usually portability is not too much of a problem but there may be times when you just need a very small amount of smoke in a different place. In this case you could use the white smoke pellet mentioned earlier, but remember if this is to be used as part of the action of the performance, it has to be lit and, once burning, will continue until it's burnt out, so the effect is not very controllable.

Back to smoke machines. There are a few small smoke machines which although needing a mains supply in order to heat to their operating temperature, have their smoke fluid pressurised into an aerosol canister so the mains supply is not needed for them to operate. Therefore they can be carried around issuing smoke as you walk along, which can be very effective where you need to have a directed layer of smoke over the acting area to reveal the effect, just prior to the curtains opening.

So for this, and lots of other smoke related effect requirements, most people would assume that if you want the smoke to appear at a distance from the static location of a smoke machine you simply use a duct or flexible hose to send the smoke to wherever you need it. Unfortunately, due to the laws of physics, it's not quite as simple as that. Air pressure build up inside the duct or hose will make it almost impossible to achieve any useful output of smoke, beyond about 3m (10ft), even when using something like a 100mm (4") ducting. You will also need to leave a small 50mm (2") airway between your smoke machine output nozzle and the start of your ducting hose. Even this arrangement will only give you a moderate distance over which you can duct your smoke – around 3m – and since even a standard smoke machine will give you an output of at least that distance, there's no great reason in going to all the effort involved. Of course there are ways of ducting your smoke over greater

Smoke machine with aerosol canister.

distances, but this will involve inducing an airflow into the duct by using a fan to draw the air and smoke along the length of the duct. This is achieved by placing the fan at the output end – in effect drawing the smoke through the duct rather than trying to push it through from the smoke machine end.

Various manufacturers will offer one or two little extras when it comes to the fluid used in their own branded machines. Some can supply you with an additive which when used mixed with their fluids will produce a scented effect. There are quite a few options available. Others offer a fluid called 'stage and studio' which dissipates about twice as fast as standard types. This is very popular with film and TV studios, where studio 'downtime' in waiting for smoke to clear can be very expensive.

The one thing common to all manufacturers, as I made comment about at the beginning of this section, is that all the smoke produced in all smoke machines is white, so if you need it to be coloured, you will have to rely on your lighting.

Another similar type of smoke effect is 'dry ice'. This is not in fact a true 'smoke' at all, but white vapour produced when dry ice (solid carbon dioxide (CO_2) comes into contact with water. It's a great effect, difficult to produce by other means, but not impossible. I'll come back to this a little later. The problems with it are the hazards involved, taking us back again to those Health and Safety issues.

Solid CO_2 or, as we all know it, dry ice, is not very friendly stuff in its solid form. It's -275 deg C and will freeze human flesh, producing dry ice burns if you touch it without protective gloves and clothing. So just handling it is not easy and neither is storing it, because it's colder than the inside of your average domestic freezer, and since it will contaminate foodstuffs you shouldn't expect to keep it there. But if you do, make sure there is no food in the freezer and turn it off, so that it's acting as a large cold box. Also, make sure your cold box or freezer doesn't have a latching lid or door. This is especially important if you are using the smaller picnic style cold box, because as the dry ice deteriorates – which it will do even inside a cold box - it gives off CO_2 gas. If stored in a sealed container, eventually the gas build up will split it open or force

A 'Peasouper' dry ice machine with ducting.

the door open. All this is before you get anywhere near to creating an effect!

The major effect from dry ice is that the vapour, which is heavier than air, sinks to the floor and depending upon the airflow present in the performance space and the amount of dry ice used, will produce a low fluffy white carpet of almost cloud-like vapour. CO_2 gas, the product of dry ice immersed in water, is present in the normal air we breath, but only in very small quantities - something like 0.2%. So as you can see, a quantity pumped into your performance space could be a dangerous thing, especially where the acting company will be working in the area for any sustained period of time. This fact, coupled with those Health and Safety regulations, has been responsible for a change in the way we regard and use dry ice. Take for example a traditional style proscenium arch theatre with an orchestra pit. Many of these older type of venues will more than likely have a raked stage, sloping from back to front, so when dry ice is used on stage, the colourless, odourless CO_2 gas and not just the white vapour that you can see, ends up down in the orchestra pit with obvious health-hazards to the musicians.

When all these handling and use issues are understood, you finally get to creating the effect, which in itself carries yet another hazard, because you are going to have large quantities of water heated to quite high temperatures, mixing with dry ice on the performance floor. This mixing obviously takes place within a dedicated dry ice machine, but you will find that no matter how watertight the actual machine is and no matter how careful you are, inevitably you will end up with water on the floor, so you have yet another potential hazard (slipping) to contend with. Just like the pyrotechnics covered previously, it may look as if I'm making a case against the use of dry ice and trying to put you off making use of this great effect, but again I stress I'm simply trying to make you aware of some of the pitfalls. If you are aware of these and plan accordingly, it will help you create your desired effect without too many problems.

One final point about dry ice, and yes, I'm afraid it's another safety issue. You will have probably seen effects created with dry ice in smaller quantities than a whole stage full: all sorts of things from the witches' cauldron in the opening scene of *Macbeth* to the foaming frothing glass of a medicinal potion, used for comic effect in countless productions. These things, especially the glass, are carefully staged effects and the prospect of one of your acting company swallowing a piece of dry ice does not bear thinking about. It's not like ordinary ice – it won't just melt away in your mouth, throat or stomach –

well not fast enough to prevent internal dry ice burning. Dry ice is very dangerous!

Right at the start of the section on dry ice I made mention about an alternative means of achieving the dry ice effect – the carpet of low lying white vapour.

Sometimes called the *cooled smoke* or *low smoke* effect, there are a number of machines available which use very high output smoke machines in which the smoke created by the use of a specific type of smoke fluid is passed through a high powered chiller unit which is an integral part of the machine. This makes the smoke lie on the floor as it's much colder than the room air temperature that it's being fed into, so it mimics dry ice but doesn't actually use any, or output any CO_2 at all.

As ever, there is a downside to this relatively new technology: the physical size of the machine and its cost. Don't expect to go and collect one of these machines from your local rental company and put it in the boot of you car – it won't fit. A small van might do but you will need two or three people to lift it in, and the cost? To hire for one week, in excess of £100; and should you want to buy one, in excess of £7,000. The price of your special effects can sometimes be very high!

Liverpool
Community
College

3 THE PROJECTED IMAGE

I'm going to concentrate on just two formats of projection in this section: gobos and the projected moving image. I'm deliberately not going to deal with slide projection or video projection, which tend to be regarded as audio-visual effects and as such are a different area of specialisation.

Gobos

The use of a metal or glass plate, etched or coloured, with the selected image for use within a profile lantern, effectively turns your lantern into a projector.

The term *gobo* is somewhat undefined in its origin. Most people believe it is a derivation of *goes before* but I have to say I have never been able to nail the exact origin of the term – perhaps someone will let me know? Or maybe there is a Mr & Mrs Gobo out there who would like to lay claim to it? Anyway, they add another dimension to the use of your lighting equipment.

The gobo will normally be fitted into a gobo holder, giving you the opportunity to rotate it at various angles to suit the requirements of the image. For first-time users, don't forget that you will be dealing with a reversed image – but you will soon get used to that. Not surprisingly you will find the size of the projected image corresponds approximately to the coverage provided by your profile lantern – so in some applications you will use a wide angle lantern and in others a standard or narrow angle.

There are at least two ways in which the gobo projected image can be used. The first and most obvious is the actual image output, visible on whatever projected surface is selected. The second are the shafts of light, in an almost laser-like quality, seen in mid-air where the projected image itself is often of no consequence. This effect is best used in conjunction with a haze machine, covered in the smoke machine section of this book, in order to make the air 'dirty' and thus show up the beams of light created by the gobo. This latter method will also benefit from the use of rotating gobos, but more of them later.

From various manufacturers there are catalogues containing literally thousands of different gobo images, so whether you are looking for a palm tree, a fleecy cloud, a happy birthday logo or an image of the Eiffel Tower, you will probably be able to choose something from an existing list. You can of course have your own design or message made into a gobo, or you could have a go at making your own, although it's doubtful that you will achieve the level of detail that you will find in the manufactured gobo ranges.

The simple gobo is the standard metal type and these come in a range of sizes, classified by letters A, B, C, M etc, offering 10 or more sizes. Each size is designed to operate in a specific type of profile lantern, or to be more precise, within a specific *gate* size. The gate is the circular aperture at

A standard metal gobo by Rosco.

the start of the lens tube of the profile lantern: i.e. between the lamp and the lenses. The gate will have small metal runners that allow you to drop in your gobo holder, complete with gobo.

The first thing to get right is the choice of the correct gobo size, and this is not always as simple as you may think, because quite a few lanterns will in fact take more than one size of gobo or even gobo holder. For example, some manufacturers will produce both an A and B size holder that will fit into most lanterns; similarly a B or M size holder. Your choice will be dependent on several factors, not least what gobo you may have available at the time – although the largest sizes simply won't fit into some profile lanterns, of course.

The gobo size is generally referenced to the diameter of the lantern's gate. However, the problem being that if you use an oversized gobo, say an A size, which will physically fit into your lantern, you run the risk of losing the projected image at the very edge of the gobo; whereas a B size, being smaller, will project the complete image of the gobo. Now this isn't quite the disaster that it might be, because for quite a lot of gobos – things like random patterns and nondescript shapes – you may not be too bothered about losing part of the image, whereas if you have a text message or a complete specific shape in your gobo, you could well end up with 'appy Birthda' or the image of a person but with no head or feet – I'm sure you can see the pitfalls!

Having selected the right size of gobo, fitted it into the holder, dropped it into the gate of your profile lantern and taken it out a few times so you can rotate it to the desired angle, you've probably burnt your fingers in the process! You will now have reached the point where you need to focus the lantern to get the best results from the gobo. Leaving aside for just a minute the actual positioning of the lantern and what you are projecting the image onto, there are two critical adjustments to be made within the lantern: the lenses and the field adjustments. I said 'lenses' inferring more than one, as you can use a gobo in a profile with a single lens, such as the old style Pattern 23, but most gobo applications work best in a lantern with two lenses, generically known as *zoom* profiles, and to get to the really high end of gobo projection performance, a condenser lens profile lantern should be used. The condenser lens is an additional lens sitting just in front of the lamp and before the gate aperture into the lens tube.

Concentrating on the zoom profile lantern, the two lenses will provide the ability to change the size of the image and also to bring the image into clear focus by the adjustment of the lens focus controls on the lens tube of the lantern. The other adjustment to be made is to the field setting, which positions the lamp in relation to the reflector: at one extreme this will produce a light output with a very intense centre 'hot spot' and at the other it will spread the light over the whole area of the output. This is known as the flat field setting and generally it's this setting which is used for gobos, since you will probably want to see the whole gobo image projected at the same intensity.

You may find that the focus of your gobo image cannot be made uniform right across the image, despite adjusting the lens focus controls: you simply can't get it focused with 100% clarity. This is not unusual. Remember you are really cheating the system here; you are trying to achieve a clear projected image with a device (profile lantern) that was built for another purpose, so as ever there has to be a trade-off in performance.

Try setting the focus to give the best overall result, then slowly bring your hand up, just in front of the lantern into the light path, and watch the result in your projected image. You will probably find that the image will get noticeably clearer but the downside to this is that you will lose a little light output, so you will need to decide what's more important – better clarity or more light. Of course you can't stand there with your hand in front of the lantern. However, there are one or two ways to overcome this problem. There is a product known as *black wrap* which is like an industrial grade of kitchen baking foil but it's black not silver. It's not cheap, but with care it should be re-useable. You can cut it into strips and because of the stiffness of the material, you can mould and fit it onto the front of your lantern, effectively replacing the masking that you achieved with your hand. Alternatively, you could try the use of a barndoor. Normally they are never used on profile lanterns for the masking properties that it brings to the Fresnel or prism convex lanterns in the same product range that it was designed for, but for some types of profile lantern, there simply may be no barndoor that is designed to fit. The barndoor idea is not likely to be as good as black wrap, because you have less adjustment opportunity. Finally, I have known lots of users who solve this problem by the deft use of a few well placed strips of gaffer tape. You must understand that I can't promote this idea, because although it's usually cheap and available, it's not designed for use in this way, mindful of the heat involved at the front end of the lantern.

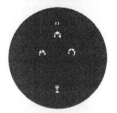

So you now have a projected gobo image to which you can add colour, just as you would in ordinary lantern use, but that's not the end of the gobo effect – far from it. Still within the simple metal gobo ranges, there are composite gobos. These are sets of two, three or more gobos which combine to make up a complete image. Within the composite selections available there are two types. There are what may be called static image composites, such as the quite famous stained glass window made up of five individual gobo images, each one intended for use in a different colour; and there are the dynamic image types, such as the water fountain, where the three gobo images are used in lanterns connected to different dimmer circuits, so that with a little careful plotting of the lighting cues (actually a chase effect) the water element appears to move and flow. These composites can be very effective but they need some very careful planning, because to really work well the multiple light sources – the lanterns – really have to be in the same place. In practical terms that means getting the lanterns as close together as possible, sometimes not as easy as it may sound.

Beyond the composites there are even more effects available, for in place of the regular gobo holder, you could choose to use a gobo rotator. This device, either in a fixed

The five elements of the DHA composite stained glass window gobo set.

speed or variable speed format, makes the image spin. OK, so you may have to work a little to find somewhere to use this in most applications, but when you need it, and often in multiples, it is very eye catching and therefore effective.

My last comment, about use in multiples, is in itself often a major cause for concern, especially to the user who has limited resources such as a relatively small quantity of lanterns and dimmer control channels. It is true that the use of the gobo projected image can be of major benefit to the production, however it's probably far cheaper and a good deal more effective to project the image of a palm tree onto a plain cyclorama cloth than to build a scenic tree, or paint a separate cloth. So, providing you keep all the production requirements in mind, you should have no problem in getting a great effect from a few well-chosen gobos. But in performance lighting design terms you probably can't have too much of a good thing – and where gobos are concerned they are even more effective when used in multiples. Some years ago I was responsible for the design and operation of a fashion show in which there were 120 gobos, and by default almost that many dimmer channels associated with them. Rather over the top? Maybe, but the effect was fantastic and of course in that particular environment budgets and similar restraints were not an issue.

Problems for the small-scale user will arise when carried away with the success and effectiveness of a few gobos, because they can multiply, and although they do indeed create some wonderful images, the real problem is that most of the available lanterns and a good number of dimmer channels are taken up in gobo work. This often results in not enough general coverage lighting left to actually 'light' the production – so be careful you don't get too carried away!

I have been describing the standard metal gobo as simple, but less so are the mesh tone and glass types. The mesh tone gobo offers a slightly higher level of definition, especially for delicate images such as clouds. The glass gobo provides one important and major attribute – the inclusion of colour. The glass used is a special heat resistant type, so don't be tempted to experiment with your own home made attempts. The thickness of the glass means that a different gobo holder

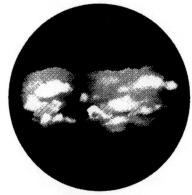

A DHA mesh gobo for tonal clouds.

A Rosco glass gobo providing a more intricate patten.

must be used and the metal and glass types of holder are not interchangeable, so don't try to use your gobo in the wrong holder. It won't work. The metal gobo in a glass holder will not be gripped and therefore will move around in the holder and the glass gobo just won't fit into a metal type holder.

Most users of the glass gobo will take the cautionary step of warming up the gobo by turning on the lantern to an imperceptibly low level before it's actually used at full light output. This will help to prevent cracked gobos, often an important factor when you consider that some multi-coloured gobos can cost hundreds of pounds to produce. The modern ranges of 'cool beam' axial profile lanterns are ideal for use with glass gobos because of the reduced heat at the lantern's gate position.

ImagePro

I started this section saying I was going to describe gobos and the projected moving image, but there is actually something else and I suppose it must have a classification all of its own because its not a gobo and although it is projected it doesn't move! Confusing? Well for many years lots of people have been trying, without much success, to use something like an ordinary acetate photographic slide in a profile lantern in the way that a gobo is used. The benefits are obvious. In the modern age of the digital image and with desktop editing available to all, the ability to capture an image of your choice and then project it into your performance event provides vast possibilities. Much of the technology has been around for a while, the trick has been to find a way of making the last important part work – getting the image to sustain the extreme temperatures of a performance lantern. In this the lantern

Rosco ImagePro.

manufacturers have been a major factor because most now build a lantern range using what is known as 'cool beam technology'. As mentioned for use with the glass gobo, this is a combination of lamp, reflector and actual lantern design, the result being that the temperature at the critical position – the lantern 'gate' where the gobo is inserted – is greatly reduced. The final part and the piece of equipment that brings us something new is the 'ImagePro' from Rosco.

The ImagePro actually describes itself as a gobo slide projector, but forgetting the gobo in its traditional form, what you get and what it's really used for is the ability to project a slide or acetate based image. The unit is a little like an extended gobo holder, dropping into the lantern gate and having a small fan module fitted on top of it which induces a cooling air flow across the acetate. The acetate slide is actually loaded into a small cartridge that fits into the ImagePro unit. The cartridge contains a clear heat resistant film also reflecting some of the infrared properties of the light beam, which sandwiches the acetate image, locating it into the optimum position within the lantern's gate aperture.

So there you have it, at last a way of getting your own photo images projected into your performance space. There is also a library of images available from Rosco, which you can buy from www.rosco.com in the same way that you can buy gobos, but of course being slides on acetate you get the added bonus of colour images. When used with the new cool beam technology profile lanterns you should get between 15 – 50 hours of use before the image starts to degrade. You can purchase the ImagePro cartridge separately, so you can make up your images ready for use. All you will need is an ink jet printer and a polyester transparency. As with all things, the higher quality of the image, printer and transparency, the better the end product effect will be.

The Projected Moving Image

There has been in existence for many years a range of moving effects, traditionally used in performance works. These effects rely upon three main elements of equipment: a high output projector, a moving effect disc and a lens.

For those of you who have not had any experience with this equipment and are possibly planning to make use of it in your next production, let me offer a few words of caution. It's not likely to be quite what you may expect! Indeed you may even be rather disappointed with the effect. At first glance of both the equipment and the specifications of it, you will probably not see a problem, after all you are starting off with a projector with a light output of 2 to 2.5kW (depending on the lamp used) so you would expect it to be really bright. That's where the problem begins, because the actual light output will not come anywhere near your expectations. That's not to say it's a bad effect or a waste of your time, far from it, but you will need to use it in the right way to get the best results from it.

When you take a closer look at those three elements of the projector, effect and lens, you will see just why the light output is so 'poor'. Within the projector itself, in front of the light source you have two large (thick) condenser lenses, then a layer of heat resistant glass, followed by yet another condenser lens; then you come to the effect itself, all the variations of which are

Strand Patt 252 effects projector with rotating disk effect.

set into a glass disc which rotates to produce the moving effect. Some of these effects such as snow and especially rain are very dark indeed because as you can imagine, it's only the snowflakes or the raindrops that need to get projected. The clouds and the flames are a little better, but still fairly dark. Then finally you come to the lens, mounted on the front of the effects disc. Having started off with a minimum of 2kW of light, by the time it's travelled through all those lenses what you are left with equates to something like a torch with a failing battery! Perhaps I exaggerate a little too much but as I said, what you often get is not what you would expect.

So why do we bother with this type of effect? After all, they're big, heavy, expensive to hire and even more so to buy, so surely there must be something better? Well actually, not much, unless you have the budget to move up to the really serious projectors with light outputs of 4kW and above, and with costs to match.

You have to remember that in general, where you are using this type of effect in your stage production, you are doing so with one important element of projection missing: a screen which in normal projection applications will give an optimum surface on which to present the image. I know that in the case of cloud projection and maybe some of the others you might be projecting onto a plain white cyclorama cloth, but even that is not the same as a real projection screen, and for other applications such as a whole area covered in snow or rain, there is no screen at all, just a big open space full of scenery and people. This fact, coupled with the poor light output of the projector, explains the reason for the apparent poor performance of the effect. So what's the solution?

It's quite simple really, and fairly easy to achieve – less light. By that I mean less *ambient* light. We know that we aren't going to get much light out of our projector, so we need to reduce the amount of light in the space that we are going to project into. For things like snow and rain, look at your effect in a completely blacked out area – then you might start to be impressed. Of course it's not realistic to expect the effect lighting to be the only source of light, after all, the audience does need to see the performers and not just your effect. You will need to start adding in a general or specific area lighting coverage, to a point where your performance space is lit and the effect is still visible – a fine balancing act. I said this was "fairly easy to achieve", well technically it probably is, assuming you have any normal type of dimmer system in place to reduce the overall light levels. The difficulty you are likely to have is with your producer or director who, not understanding the technical side of things, will expect a stage full of lighting with a raging snow blizzard imposed on top of it! If this is the case then you are probably using the wrong effect (or producer or director!). See the dynamic effect section later in this book for more information on this subject.

You will find that it's rare for just one moving effect projector to provide the complete effect that you need as they work best in multiples – which in itself must help matters because you will be multiplying the light output.

There are generally only three or four lens variations available for your projected effect, starting with the 2½", the widest angle available, and through to the 3" and 4", and up to the 6" which is narrowest. You will probably have noted the reference to inches – which gives you some idea of how long these effects have been around – approaching 50 years now, which makes them almost antique!

One thing which has changed for the better recently is the advent of a better motor control and the application of the ubiquitous DMX control protocol. Indeed this is the only format now available, but I'm sure that there will be lots of the older style units still out there somewhere, so I urge you to keep your sanity, and if you are going to hire or borrow a moving effect, make sure it's one of the modern types. Otherwise you can look forward to motors running at different speeds which on clouds on a backcloth or snow all over your stage which can look very odd, or, worse still, motors sticking or even going into reverse!

I said these things were big and heavy and so they are, probably weighing in excess of 30kg. Therefore you will need to think carefully about how and where you mount them. Being at least a 2kW lamp (2.5kW in the most modern projectors types) you must also consider what you are connecting them into and I don't just mean the dimmer. At 2kW, that's a shade under 9 Amps, so for any of you who are running on old 5 amp installations, don't try using them, as they will overload your wiring and connectors, heat them to a point of meltdown and could start a fire! As you can see from the load involved, even where you are using a 15 amp installation which will cope happily with the load involved, you can only use one projector on one dimmer if they are standard 10 Amp dimmers.

For the projected moving image of clouds running across your back cloth or cyclorama, even the smallest of stages will probably need two units, and the location of these will be critical to the success of the effect. It needs to be around three to four metres maximum in front of the cloth and sited so that the projected image has the shallowest of angles onto it, because what you are projecting has no keystone correction and if the angle is too steep you will have difficulty in getting a good overall focus of the image. The keystone effect is probably less critical for other effects in the range, but its affect on your projected image should not be ignored.

There are a few small accessories that you might find useful, in the application of your projected effect.

The Masking Plate Shutter

This is a simple metal plate with four moveable metal sections, which gives you the ability to set a masked area: sides, top and bottom. It's a little like the masking shutters of a profile lantern or the barndoor on a Fresnel lantern. The masking shutter fits into a carrier slot, just behind the lens on the front of the effects disc, and it's a trial and error operation to adjust and set it to the required positions.

The Beam Diversion Mirror

This does just what it says: it clips onto the front of the lens and can divert to image to any angle of your choice up to 90 degrees. This allows you to position a projector directly above an area and have the image projected onto the floor directly below, while keeping the lantern and effect at the optimum operating position. You may struggle a little to find an instant use for this particular accessory, but believe me when you need one, it's the only thing that will solve your problem.

The Slide Carrier

This actually replaces the effect disc altogether and gives you the opportunity to project a static slide. The rainbow quadrant is probably the most well known; indeed there aren't actually many other off-the-shelf slides that you can find these days. Most people who have a need to use the projector in this way will have their own slides made up. They are 3¼" square, and the carrier will hold two, with the ability to change between them. The same lens as used on the moving effect disc is used on the slide carrier and no, you can't use a domestic type 35mm slide because it won't fit in the carrier and even if it did, the heat and light output form the projector would melt it.

To summarise, the following effects are available for the moving effects projector: fleecy clouds, thunder or storm clouds, snow, rain, flames, monochrome flames (sometimes used as water) and smoke, sometimes referred to as vapour trail. Just to confuse the issue, there is also the up and down sea wave, the confusion being that this effect is not in a circular disc housing like all the others – it's in a rectangular box that sits on the front of the projector and contains photographic slide images of sea waves that are moved up and down in conjunction with a piece of break-up glass. The end result is really very good and even quite bright compared to most of the other effects, but as with all these things, it's a one off. How often do you actually need an image of waves in your production?

So that's about it for the projected moving effect. Certainly in the old conventional style they are cumbersome, heavy, expensive, time consuming, and a fiddle to set up. In short they are a real pain, but when you get them set up correctly and used in the right conditions, despite

Strand Lighting's up and down sea wave effect attachment.

their age and rather low-tech ability, they still produce a great effect.

So what about the new convention of the projected moving image? Well, there are at least two manufacturers who are developing a product that could supersede the traditional dedicated projector and motorised effect disc. These systems, which are really still in their development, work in a different way.

The light source is a high power CDM lamp (a discharge lamp) used in a traditional profile lantern housing, using a dichroic reflector and what is called cool beam technology. This reduces the level of heat passing through the lantern gate, while still maintaining a very high light output. The projected image is contained on an acetate thin film sheet that is passed across the gate – a little like the colour gel string in a colour scroller. Added to this is the lens, with all the variations found in the modern profile lantern ranges, a mechanical shutter to provide a dimming facility (remember because it's a discharge lamp you can't control it with your normal dimmer) and of course DMX control to govern the speed of the effect and the opening and closing of the shutter. This new advance has the potential to provide a new and vast array of different moving images: in fact, any photographic image that can be transferred to the acetate film. We may be a little way off seeing it in regular and easily obtainable use just yet, but it's coming!

The Moving Head Lantern

I confess I have a personal problem with automated luminaires, on many fronts. However, I'm including them here because, even though these lanterns have

The Martin Mac 250 – a typical moving head fixture.

been generally accepted into the performance lighting list of equipment, I still regard them as 'effect' lanterns. You will probably know that they exist in both the Fresnel and profile versions and many designers and users are now regarding them as "all that's needed to light your stage". That's the main problem I have with them. I'm not saying there's anything wrong with them, far from it. The abilities they bring are fantastic; it's just that in lots of lighting applications the actual movement of the light is, for me, a distraction. Yes, of course, in the right piece of theatre and certainly in modern music performance events, they are the norm – however, not in every style of performance. Their use is becoming more widespread and as I said, regarded as an effect, they are great.

So what is there to know about these moving head lanterns? For a start let me make just one major point. I'm talking about moving head lanterns, where the whole lantern body moves, not a moving mirror lantern, where the body of the lantern is static and a mirror in front of the lens reflects the light to different positions. In my book these are 'disco fittings' and have very little, if any, place in theatrical lighting.

Concentrating on the moving head profile version, this type of lantern provides a number of functions not found in ordinary profile lanterns:

1. the motorised ability to vary the beam angle, to make the light output beam bigger or smaller
2. to add a gobo from a pre-loaded selection
3. to add and change colour
4. the whole lantern is mounted within a motorised yoke that you can program into virtually any position.

You would think that with so many fabulous attributes that's it, lighting job done. Well as I've said, for some event and presentation work they are fine, but their use in the more traditional stage performance is perhaps not so easy to define, let's list a few of their drawbacks:

- They are heavy (25-35kgs)
- They will need a dedicated mains power supply (not via your dimmer)
- They will each need a dedicated DMX 512 control signal (actually using 7 or more DMX channels)
- They will probably need a dedicated moving light orientated control desk (if your existing control desk won't support them)
- Their use will probably require an experienced operator, to set up and program them (if you are inexperienced and do it yourself, expect many hours of toil!)
- They are expensive (to buy and hire)
- They really work best in multiples and I don't mean two or three, but six or 12 would have an impact.

You have probably worked out by now that these fixtures are not for the low budget low-tech event; they take time, money and a good deal of effort to get into your production and at the end of all that, they are, for me, just an effect. Granted, they are a very good effect that you can't replicate any other way, but an effect nonetheless. So since this is *basics*, I'm going to stop there with this particular range of special effects.

The Animation Disc

Something else that creates an effect but is actually an accessory, rather than equipment such as the moving effect projector, is the animation (or break-up) disc. I suggest that to get the real benefit form this effect, you really do need to use it in multiples. It's rare to find an application where just one unit on its own can produce a noticeable effect, but I'm sure there must be one.

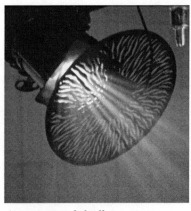

An animation disk effect.

The animation disc is a thin metal circular disc, revolving on a centre spindle driven by a small motor, at either a fixed speed or a variable speed governed by an external remote controller. The discs are cut with various different patterns, each designed to give a different style of animation and here's the vital part: they are designed and intended for use on a profile lanterns using a gobo to generate the initial image.

Note I said: *"used on a profile lantern"* – not in it, because the disc slots into the colour runners right at the front of the lantern. It's not used to affect the light path within the lens structure, as with the gobo. What it's doing is a little like the sharper focus trick I described when talking about gobos, only on a more regular and larger scale, and it can be very effective when used in the correct combination of gobo and disc.

There are a wide range of applications that benefit from animation discs; flames and water are probably the most well known and most seen, but really anything can be used. I know its not a true movement – it's more like a shimmering property that's produced, which is why use in multiples tends to fool the audience into thinking that it's actually moving. That's why flames and water work so well, because we all accept that there is a large element of repetitiveness in these images. The effect of sunlight through trees is another perhaps less well known effect of this type and of course depending upon your staging, may need some help with the addition of some scenery.

Again you will need to give some careful thought to the overall lighting condition of the area when using an animated effect, although they don't suffer the poor light output problem quite as much as the moving effect projector, and the image will be governed ultimately by the power and ability of the profile lantern you are using.

The Tubular Ripple

There is one other effect which I have not classified with the projected moving effect – the tubular box ripple machine. It falls across two boundaries: yes, it's a lighting effect that does produce an element of movement, but since it has no lens or even a reflector it is not a projector in the true sense. It does one job and one job only, for which it is excellent, but again it has a limited light output, so must be used carefully within the right light conditions.

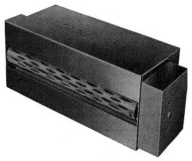

Strand Lighting tubular ripple.

It's simply a small rectangular box (about 600mm x 200mm x 250mm) which contains two 1000W linear tungsten halogen lamps working together, in front of which sits a 60mm metal cylinder punched with a regular slotted pattern that is slowly rotated by an integral low power motor. The side of the rectangle away from the lamps is opened up along its complete length, so that the light can escape. There is a set of colour runners and colour frame on the open side and small brackets at each end to provide floor mounting or suspension, with a suitable lock-off device.

What you get as light output is not adjustable; there is no lens to focus the image, no reflector and once you have dropped your chosen colour into it, that's it! You simply place it (usually on the floor) in front of your backcloth or cyclorama, and you obtain an instant water ripple effect. At about 1.5 to 2 metres you will get a coverage of about three metres wide by one metre high, so just as with the other effects, you will probably need two or more units to really make an impact.

The tubular ripple machine will normally require two power feeds, one for the lamps and one for the motor, from a constant supply. Some people are tempted to pair the feeds together and just have the whole thing under the control of a dimmer channel for convenience, but beware, if you do this you will find that the motor, not liking the chopped wave form of the dimmer circuit, will stop working at less than the maximum output of the dimmer, and somewhere in your lighting cue to fade in or fade out the effect, you will have static waves. Not a very professional piece of work!

Finally, just a couple of notes of caution where all these effects are concerned. I'm sure you have noticed that they all use a motor to drive the effect and motors make noise! And here I am telling you to use them in multiples! Well for most applications it won't be a problem, especially if you are dealing with a pantomime or musical, but just stop and consider the possible background hum that you could end up with from heavy use of these effects in a quiet, wordy dramatic piece of theatre.

In *Basics – A Beginner's Guide to Stage Lighting* I made reference to the time it takes to get the critical focus of lanterns just right. Well, effects projectors of all types are going to add to that time. Don't expect that it will be five-minute job to add the odd effect here and there, especially for the first-time user. It will take much longer than that.

4 THE DYNAMIC EFFECT

Dynamic: *Relating to motive force, in action.*

We'll forgo the obvious things such as scenic cloths or curtains, because even though they do create what to some may be regarded as a special effect, I think that most would accept that in the performance space environment these things are really the norm and therefore not 'special'.

I've also already ruled out the speciality of flying people as this really is a step too far in the realms of special effects for all but the specially trained and those suitably covered by large public liability insurance!

So what else do you use in, on and around a performance stage, that has an element of movement and can be classified as a special effect that's not a pyrotechnic or lighting effect? Well, quite a lot actually.

It seems that I spend a lot of time writing about what I'm not going to cover, and rather glossing over the effect in question, and yes, here comes another one: **the stage trap.** Well, perhaps you will forgive me this one? Yes, it is a very special effect, and really quite spectacular. But let's get realistic here; if your performance space does not have a large under-stage area and a ready-built mechanism, you are not likely to be in a position to achieve the stage trap effect. For those of you lucky enough to use a venue such as an old Victorian style theatre, then you will know that it is a special piece of equipment which requires rather a lot of manpower and special training by those who have experience of it.

By way of explanation so that those of you who still hanker after the effect can at least rule it out, let me explain the workings of these marvellous, now sadly vary rare devices.

One arrangement was called a 'star' trap, because the section of stage floor that the artiste passed through was cut in a sort of star shape and hinged in such a way that the leaves fell back into place, leaving no apparent point of entry.

I believe the more common stage trap was not fitted with such refinements as the star top, it relied on a section of the stage equal to the actual trap floor being released from its fixed position and dropping down onto timber runners and then being pulled away (sideways) leaving a square hole in the stage floor,

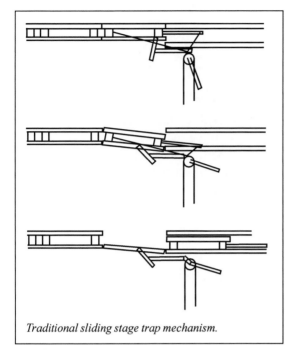

Traditional sliding stage trap mechanism.

this action was timed a few seconds before the artiste on the trap floor below was hurtled upwards through the hole and onto the stage. The trap floor now became the stage floor, and would either stay in position waiting for the artiste to make a return trip back downwards, or, as soon as the artiste had stepped off, it would be lowered and the original stage floor section slid back and locked in place.

That briefly describes the action involved but comes nowhere near describing the actual trap machinery or the choreographed actions of the six people it took to work it under stage. These are examples of Victorian ingenuity in the use of woodwork, pulley and counterweight systems. They worked, they were very efficient, and very fast when worked by an experienced crew, but really quite dangerous if you got it wrong. But the spectacle of seeing a scene in a pantomime using two standard traps, a grave trap and a set constructed with secret revolving door panels and walls that you could walk through, used by experienced artistes, was something that thrilled generations of theatre audiences. Maybe one day someone will realise how good it was as an effect, and re-invent it. I hope so. But in the meantime I don't think this is something you will be able try out.

But a dynamic effect that most people can use is the **snow bag** or snow cloth (for snow you can substitute leaves or whatever takes your fancy). It's the low-tech and usually fool proof way of getting a simulated snow effect to fall all over your stage. Well perhaps not quite all of it, but enough to fool your audience.

I confess it does work best over a proscenium arch stage and, as you will see, would have its limitations in other performance spaces. It also relies upon having at least a means of suspension above the stage area – but then if you are performing on a proscenium arch stage you will probably have that anyway.

I do make the point regularly, when engaged in the topic of theatre performance space design, that, in my opinion, a 'proper' theatre has a fly tower and theatres built without a fly tower only have a suspension system, but I must try not to get side tracked into all that, or this book could end up like War and Peace!

The suspension system will give you a means of raising and lowering the snow bag on two independently controlled sets of flying lines. To clarify, a *set* is usually made up of three individual lines (sometimes more) which used all together connected to a bar or wooden batten will raise and lower it to the required height. It will normally tie off at a cleat traditionally located on the fly rail

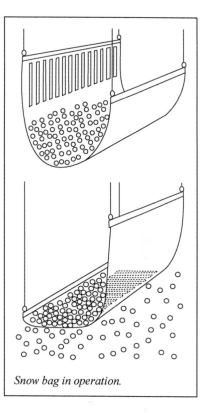

Snow bag in operation.

but in some applications it may be at a side wall position at side stage level. The bar or batten will traverse the width of the stage more or less to the extent of the proscenium opening.

The snow bag is not actually a bag at all, but simply a cloth, about two or three metres deep and the length of the proscenium opening. It will have tape ties along each long edge and one edge will be tied to one suspension bar the other to another bar, the bars being quite close together so that when they are level the cloth hangs down in a 'U' shape – and it's within this 'U' shape that the snow, leaves, or whatever is placed. You can buy polystyrene snow beads, white confetti, or make your own variation of whatever works as snow in your space. Then by the action of raising one of the bars and leaving the other one in a static position, the contents of the snow bag will spill over and fall out.

There you have it, an instant look-alike snow effect. There is a small refinement that will help: cut a series of vertical slits (note slits, not holes) all along the top edge of the cloth, extending about 500mm down from the static suspension bar, so that when the snow is rolled onto the slitted section by the raising action of the other bar, the snow falls through the slits rather than pouring over the static bar. A little practice in the action of raising the bar will produce the magical effect – the downside to which is the mess that it creates on the stage floor. You also have the risk factor as mentioned with the confetti cannon, where re-useable snow can contain various foreign bodies that you really don't want falling onto your acting company, because apart from having to make repetitive entries in the accident book, which will read rather oddly as "cut head by falling snow effect", actually looks very odd to the audience when the lightweight snow is interspersed with heavier objects falling noticeably faster and making a noise as they hit the floor, or the performers! Have fun with your snow bag – it's another one of those lovely low-tech things that is fairly cheap and easy to set up and gives a great effect.

There is, as you would imagine, a 21st century version of the snow bag, the falling snow machine. This is a two metre long trough that can be used in multiples end to end, suspended above the performance stage and filled with polystyrene snow beads. Electrically operated on cue, it will sprinkle snow at the touch of a button. Each two metre section is heavy (25kgs+) so its application in your space may not be simple. But at the other end of the spectrum, where maybe you just need a dusting of snow to cover your actor before making an entrance, then off stage you can use the **snow in a can** – a small aerosol that will do the job. Just don't get it mixed up with fly spray or the WD40!

Along the same budget-conscious lines as the snow bag here's another cheap

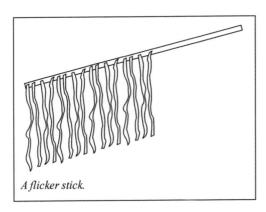

A flicker stick.

and very simple thing to make an effect – **the flicker stick** – used to create the impression of flames. Actually it's a lighting effect, but it's the flicker stick that makes it work. The requirement is usually to simulate flames or a fire effect, within a small specific area. Again, you may have to think a little about just how and where you use it, maybe in a fire backing of a fireplace within a room set, or perhaps a door backing simulating flames in a room off stage. You will need two or three 500W lanterns: Fresnel and profile. You will need two profiles if you are using three lanterns using the Fresnel to focus a wide area coverage, probably with a dark to medium amber colour, and the profile or profiles to be more tightly focused onto the specific area, just out of a hard focus, probably using a red and or different colour amber to the Fresnel. Obviously all these lanterns are set up off stage out of view, then you need the 'flicker stick', a small piece of wood about a metre long and quite thin (half of an old broom handle would be fine) and then some strips of old material. Anything that's available: old dusters, rags, strips of canvas, which with a few small tacks or a staple gun, you attach to the first 500mm of your stick. The strips need to be 600 – 700mm long, but this is not an exact piece of equipment, so don't worry about any detailed measurements.

Then simply hold the stick so that the strips of material are in front of your profile lantern and start flickering. Practice – trial and error will show you what gives the best effect and you can amend and change the fabric strips, even the length of the stick, to suit your needs. It does have one downside though. It's OK for a short-lived simulation, but it's not very clever if you have to sustain it for half an hour! You will need to combine your physical efforts with a little help from a lighting cue, maybe even a small chase set up on the dimmers controlling the lanterns. You could go to the super deluxe version and use a flame gobo in one or both of your profile lanterns, but it works quite well without. Try it. It's a simple low-cost, even no-cost effect.

Something not quite so simple and definitely not a home-made effect, is the **breakaway**, commonly seen as a bottle being smashed over someone's head. They are is available in a wide range of shapes and sizes, although the ubiquitous wine or beer bottle is the most common and most readily available. These are made from a resin compound, dyed brown or green or left clear, and the bottle variations are even supplied with a stick-on label, or of course you could make your own.

The breakaway is also available in sheet form, to simulate a pane of glass, where it is commonly known as *sugar glass*. In this form it starts to get rather expensive and not very readily available, but if the action calls for someone getting thrown though a window, then that's what you need.

The big problem with all breakaways is that they are extremely fragile and I do mean *extremely.* They are a real nuisance to transport and many companies won't want to handle them because the breakage rate before they get anywhere near an end-user is so high, and even when you have gone to collect them carefully from a supplier, I'll guarantee that a fair proportion will not make it to your production in one piece.

There is also a little artistic licence involved in the use of breakaways – take the standard bottle for instance. When you do actually manage to crack it over someone's head it neither looks or sounds quite as you would expect, but then I don't suppose many of us have been in close proximity to the real thing anyway and as it's such an instant, split second effect, perhaps I'm being a little too critical.

Even the standard bottle is not a cheap effect at something over £10 plus the breakages likely to be involved, but if you need one, it's the only thing I know of that will do the job.

The **Gauze Transformation** is not so much a case of what you need, although the correct equipment is vital, but rather a case of just how you use it to create one of the classic effects in a theatrical performance. In its smallest and simplest form let's start off with a portrait or picture and assume it to be life size. This will need to face your audience full on, not at an angle, as this will present the best transformation effect to the most people, and even those seated to one side of your auditorium should see the effect, although with a slightly degraded end product. The actual position of your portrait and the construction of it will need to take into consideration just what the action calls for. If it were just a transformation in which the portrait comes to life, but stays within the portrait frame, then that's quite simple. However, if the action requires that the now lifelike 'real' person walks out of the portrait and into the action on stage, that's a slightly different matter, so let's deal with the simple one first.

Of course your portrait will be a gauze cloth and the grade of gauze will determine just how good the effect is. Don't get too carried away with the selection of the gauze, a standard sharkstooth scenic gauze should be fine. Anyway, since you are only dealing with a relatively small area, you could experiment with a number of gauze densities and choose the one that works best for your needs. The gauze will be stretched over a portrait-sized frame and tacked or stapled in place. Because it's gauze and not a fabric with a 100% weave density, you will probably find that you have to use a some form of stiffener at the point of attachment. Laths of thin timber may do the job or anything to ensure that the gauze stays taught over the frame. In this format you need to get the portrait image applied to the gauze. Note that I didn't say *painted*, although if you are careful about your choice of paint type and how it's applied, it can work. More often it's not a paint that's used, but a dye that colours the gauze material, but unlike regular paint does not fill up the holes which are the main feature of the gauze and what you need to have in place to make your transformation work.

Then with a suitable picture frame fitted for the benefit of the audience, your portrait can be positioned on the wall of your set, covering an opening cut out to the same size as the portrait, behind which your artiste will stand or sit. This area, which in the case of the portrait effect is quite small, is obviously outside of the main set and the backing of this area will need to be a mirror of the image in the portrait, i.e. if it were a landscape the backing would be painted in the same style and lit as part of the transformation process, however if the portrait were a figure standing in front of a dark or nondescript background, then the backing could be black and left unlit.

Of course your artiste and the portrait should contain enough similarities to convince the audience of the connection and then the effect itself is all about the lighting. For the portrait to be realistic it will need one or more lanterns focused onto it from the front, and most importantly it will need a black curtain on a track directly behind it. At the moment of the transformation, the black curtain is drawn aside and a lighting cue will bring up the lanterns behind the gauze, lighting your artiste and, if needs be, the background, in a crossfade that will remove the lanterns lighting the gauze from the front. If the action is then contained within the portrait, maybe with gestures or even small movements and dialogue, then that is the end of the effect, until it is normally reversed, leaving the portrait lit from the front again.

If the action calls for your artiste to enter onto the stage, then a little more is required. The gauze panel which is the portrait needs to be removed so that the artiste can step through the frame and onto the stage. To achieve this the whole gauze panel frame needs to be mounted on a track system, so that after the initial lighting transformation has revealed your artiste, the frame can be slid away sideways, all of this action being reversible if required. This last requirement will obviously affect just how you build the frame and gauze panel, where you mount it with regard to your artiste stepping through it, how you operate it (not left to the artiste) and even some covering business by other artistes on stage, to take the eyes of the audience away from the frame edge as it passes across the front of the artiste within the now fully lit up stage transformation area.

There's a lot of work to do to make this effect work seamlessly. It will take quite some time to rehearse and if not done correctly can look rather poor and shoddy, but when you get it just right it's a stunning effect. Even more so when you get it right on the grand scale: a full stage transformation. We have to pause here, to consider just where you can use this grand effect, and there's not much of an option. You can really only achieve it on a proscenium stage and preferably one with a full flying facility. The full flying facility is where cloths or scenery in use on stage can be flown directly upward and completely out of sight; so if your masking flats, scenery and cloths are 5.5 to 6m high, then the available flying height over stage will be more than double this. (Please refer to my note about the design of a performance spaces mentioned in the snow bag section.)

If you are working in a proscenium arch stage where flying is limited to less than full height, all is not lost, but you will need to use a special type of curtain track called a 'wipe' track to achieve the effect.

With the larger, full stage effect, you will not have the option of holding your gauze cloth in a frame. Where you have the flying facility it will be tied to a bar and the bottom of the gauze will be made with a pocket sewn into it containing a steel conduit or similar batten to provide just enough weight to keep the gauze taught.

The important black masking cloth behind the gauze will also be tied to a flying bar and the bottom of this black cloth will have a chain weight at its base.

Using this method of suspension makes the removal of these elements simple and effective. The gauze cloth may be used in its plain form, unpainted, although the effect usually has a bigger impact on the audience if the transformation is moving from one distinct scene to another. Incidentally, it's not always the case that the image on the gauze is mirrored by what is behind it, quite often it is completely different as a requirement of the transformation.

If you don't have the flying facility and need to resort to the curtain track system, then for the black masking curtain you could use a regular overlap chord-operated track, but for the gauze curtain an overlap track would mean the use of a pair of gauze curtains which would produce an overlap and central seam from top to bottom. If you can live with this, fine, but a wipe track will allow you to wipe away the one-piece gauze cloth from one side of the stage to the other – a much neater and better effect.

The principle of the lighting changes to make the transformation effect happen are the same as previously described, albeit that you are dealing with a much larger area. One thing that will accentuate the effect, apart from getting the transformation timing just right, is the level of detail put into the lighting of the gauze from the front, especially where it has an image rather than being just a plain cloth.

There are also many instances in all forms of performance works where the gauze cloth is fixed across the back of the proscenium arch and the whole production takes place behind the gauze as a sort of half complete transformation. This usually requires the use of a gauze containing lots of detail in the artwork of the image and very carefully painted or dyed and of course the lighting of the production is critical, since no front of house lighting can be used to light the stage.

The transformation effect is a classic. It can be a problem to create across all the technical disciplines involved, but when you get it right, it's a real show stopper.

Liverpool
Community
College

5 WHAT'S LEFT?

Firstly I want to deal with a few special lighting effects, and I will start with **strobes**. I think we all know what effect strobe lighting provides and there are one or two things that are an absolute 'must have' requirement for a strobe to work properly. The first and most important factor is a blackout; the

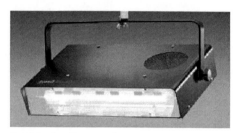

Optikinetics Terrastrobe.

second is an understanding by the users – by which I mean the producers and directors – that a good strobe effect is anything that doesn't go on too long. So how long is too long? Everybody will have their own ideas on this, but for me, it's probably something not much more than 30 seconds, and much of course will depend upon the action taking place.

You will find that most performance works and venues will advise their audience that: *"Stroboscopic lighting takes place during this production"* or other similar warning information. The reason for this, and really the reason why prolonged exposure is not a good idea, is that the rapid flashing of lights can affect the brain's wave patterns; indeed strobe lighting has been used in the treatment of epilepsy but in certain conditions, where the flashing light is set at a specific flash rate, it has been found that this can even induce an epileptic fit. Even for people not prone or affected by epilepsy, sitting in a blacked out space and having bright lights flashed rapidly on and off will soon make them feel rather uncomfortable. It's a bit like the proven methods of interrogation and sensory depravation, except or course, all in the name of entertainment! So don't overdo your strobe effects.

Blacklight, more commonly referred to as UV (*ultra violet*) is another lighting effect that some people have difficulty with. In some ways it's like strobe lighting in that it needs a blackout to work effectively, and the duration of a scene played under UV lighting can be a problem unless the content of the action is able to hold the attention of the audience. Even then, once you have been sitting in the dark for more than five minutes looking at coloured apparitions floating in mid air, the novelty starts to wear off. And, of course, especially for the performers who are actually being lit with the UV light, we are these days made aware that prolonged exposure to UV light, especially the eyes, is not good for you.

Something which is confusing to the first time user may be the reference made by other, non-performance related industries, to the type of UV light used. One of the most popular ways of achieving the UV effect on stage is by the use of the 1200mm (4ft) UV fluorescent tube fitting, and that's where the confusion starts because the UV tube used in stage performance work is different to the tube that actually carries the name UV, which is a white tube that fluoresces bright blue. It's the thing you see in sun beds and is totally useless to you in stage performance works. What you need for the stage use is a 'black light' tube. It's easy to tell apart from the other types as it's the only one that's actually black, and it also costs four times as much as the others.

Once you have this little problem out of the way, you need to consider how many black light sources you need and where to position them to give the lighting coverage of the area you are using. It seems rather strange to talk about a lighting coverage for a light that is practically invisible to the human eye, but that's what you need to think in terms of, because as with all other lighting, the effects of being in shadow and the coverage of the area are vital to the overall success of the effect. A typical requirement may be for a number of people dressed in black leotards with white skeleton bones fixed in place all over the leotard and a white skull mask. All very effective, but if you have placed your black light UV tubes down in the traditional footlight position at the front of the stage, as your skeletons move around some will move into the shadow of those in front of them, so you will probably need to have some black light fittings sited overhead to combat this problem.

There are many different colours of UV paint available, so you can make up your fish fixed to a black stick, or whatever shape or article you choose, and paint it whatever colour you want. Then it's all up the creativity of the director about how to make the best of the UV effect.

Many of you will have seen in recent years the **Practical Flame Effect.** There are a number of different options from the pyrotechnic to the wind and light combination, and it's the latter that I'm going to deal with here. We should not discount the pyrotechnic effect – it's great – but by the nature of it, you will find that it's not simple or straightforward because it will bring you into contact with your local fire officer and a whole host of rules, regulations and operational detail which are anything but *basic*.

The wind and light combination can be a really stunning effect, but the main feature of it is that it is in fact a piece of material, usually white silk. These effects are mainly quite small to be at their most effective. The base of the effect, which can be in various shapes to suit the surroundings, contains a small fan above which is fixed the piece of silk in a roughly triangular shape, pinnacle uppermost. Also contained within the base are one or two small low output lamps – the 50mm dichroic types are a favourite for this. The top of the base containing these components is left completely open and the effect is the visual aspect of the silk, seeming to flicker as flames do.

True, you can't use them in every application and yes, they do need a mains power supply to operate, but they really are very effective. Again, we have the same situation as highlighted in the moving effects – more is

A silk flame effect.

obviously a better effect, but the fans, especially in the larger units, can combine to make it rather noisy, but using three or four of the smaller units shouldn't present any problems. As with the motors in the moving effects, you may need to separate the fans from the circuits powering the lighting elements, otherwise the effect could start and stop in a rather strange way.

The **Flicker Candle** is another effect which is difficult to achieve any other way, especially since, in this day and age, the use of a real live candle on stage is bound to be frowned upon by those in control of the venue and the local fire officer.

Anyway, the vagaries of real candles and the performers who use them are good reasons for using the life-like electric type instead. Many people will make their own versions based upon torch lamps and batteries, with an off-white twist of paper wrapped around the lamp to add a touch of realism. If this method works for you with a little help from the acting company in just how they are used, then that's fine, but where you need a real look-alike candle, then the flicker candle is the thing to use.

The candle is powered by a standard 9v battery and

Flicker candle, photo: Cerebrum Lighting.

will have a switch at the base. The actual flicker effect is made by the mechanical movement of the candle flame shaped lamp, which is held in a delicate mounting so that as you move around the whole flame trembles slightly, producing the effect. So it's totally safe, it requires no mains power, and can be used singly. What could go wrong? Just make sure your candle has a good battery in it, or your performer could be responsible for a very special effect indeed, the very rare candle effect that gradually fades to extinction!

Not making a regular appearance in theatrical productions but more of a novelty effect are **Bubbles.** There are various machines on the market which with a wide range of end product availability, can produce bubbles for you. This might sound rather strange, but these things can be a real danger and not for the reason you would expect. It's back to those health and safety matters again. In a recent case-study of accidents at work (actually on building sites), the majority of accidents were caused by slips, trips and falls. So when your bubbles have had their impact, they fall to the floor and as most often the performance floor is a hard non absorbent surface and your bubble machine is likely to output a substantial quantity of potentially slippery deposits all over it, which introduces another risk.

The **Wind Machine (1)** *((2) follows later)*. As with smoke and bubbles, there are several manufacturers who make wind machines. Not massively used in theatre performance work, the small ones are no more than a domestic fan, whereas the large ones could blow your scenery over. Most offer a variable speed control and they are usually just there to add that little touch of realism, like a breeze rippling the curtains of a window in your stage set.

Don't forget that one aspect of this type of wind machine is the sound generated. This can of course be a required part of the effect, but I suggest that in most applications there will be a fine balance between wanting to 'see' the effect, but have some level of control over the sound that it creates.

The **Star Cloth.** There are two options here: the older pea lamp cloth and the more modern and much more effective fibre optic cloth. In both options the actual cloth is usually made up in a black material, since the normal function of the star cloth is to produce the image of stars in the night sky.

The pea lamp cloth, using white LES (Lilliput Edison Screw) lamps, just like the ones you find on your Christmas tree lights, offers the standard format. The density of lamps used in the make up of the cloth will dictate just how good the effect looks. Each lamp is pushed through the weave of the cloth and sewn in place and the wiring loom simply hangs to the floor on the back of the cloth where the various individual looms are wired together, giving you one connection to make to a mains power supply, probably a dimmer circuit. This type of star cloth is rather delicate and tricky to put in place, as you are constantly wrestling with the wiring looms sewn on the back of the cloth, and of course the effect you get is static pinpoints of light, all working together.

The fibre optic cloth is similar in its make up, but in place of a mains wiring loom individual strands of fibre optic cable are used and the real benefit is in how light is applied to these cables. They are all brought together into bundles, each bundle connecting to a specially adapted low light output form of projector. This normally comes as part of the star cloth and depending upon the version you buy or hire, will give you the simple static pinpoint of light, or more likely something that will change colour slightly from a cool blue to a brilliant white and make the light appear to twinkle and rise and fall in intensity. Once you have used the fibre optic version, you won't want to go back to the old pea lamp type!

The **Mirror Ball** is probably the best known special effect. Well, I'm sure we have all seen one so I don't think it needs much description from me, at least not the mirrored ball part, but what about the rotator and what lanterns will give you the best effect?

The rotator and its suspension, indeed the link between the rotator and the ball, is often a cause for concern because over the years there have been unfortunate incidents of things becoming unattached, depositing the mirror ball onto the floor and acting company below. The rotator is probably best fitted with a standard hook clamp which will allow you to suspend it from a lighting bar. This may be somewhat difficult as the majority of rotators are built into metal cases that offer fixings to a flat surface. The link between the rotator and the ball is often made with a length of chain. The critical points here are at each end: rotator and ball. Indeed, it is also wise to check the spindle and attachments on the ball itself.

Once all matters of suspension and rotation out of the way, you need to apply light to it. Here, much will depend upon the size of the venue, for if it's relatively small then the PAR36 pin spot may be all that you need, but in a larger venue you may need to use a 600 or 1200W profile lantern in order to get enough light reflecting off it. When using a profile lantern (Fresnels and prism convex lanterns really won't do) you will need to use an adjustable iris diaphragm in order to close the focus of the lantern right down to the size of the ball. Try to get your lantern fairly close to the ball: 2-3m would be good.

Also think about the effect you want to see. If you place your lantern above the centre line of the ball, then most of the effect is going to be seen coming up, reflected off the ball, whereas with the lantern below the centre line, most of the effect will be seen on the floor.

Most people regard the mirror ball as a rather old fashioned 'one trick' effect. the next time you need to use one, try multiple lanterns, two, three or even four, in different colours from different angles. Even set up as a chase on your lighting control desk – you might be surprised at the sort of effect you can create and if you really want some fun, try two mirror balls and multiple lanterns.

The **Thunder Sheet** (and here I must express a preference against this very old style effect) is simply a sheet of thin steel plate, about 2.8 x 1.4m (8 x 4ft), thin enough to have some flexibility, because the action involves hanging it up somewhere backstage so that you can hold on to the bottom of it and shake it vigorously to create the sound of thunder. My problem with it (*and I have seen and heard lots of shapes and sizes*) is that it always sounds to me like someone is shaking a piece of tin plate, and never anything quite like thunder. So I really wouldn't bother as these days a recorded sound effect will do a better job for you.

So what about recorded **Sound Effects?** Well, I suppose they are a sort of special effect but really they are a area and a discipline all to themselves.

In *Basics – A Beginner's Guide to Stage Sound*, I made some mention of sound effects in promoting the use of the modern technology available: the CD and the depth of pre-recorded effects available and the Mini Disc and its editing functions. I'm not keen to major the sound effects labelled as a special effect; it's a large topic that won't benefit from the *Basic* treatment. But there is one thing that I must promote where the sound effects are concerned and it's more to do with the equipment than the effects you can create.

The actual sound that you hear as the effect needs to be realistic for it to be effective. I know that statement may seem rather odd, but take, for example, the sound effect of a thunder storm (reference my earlier comments about the thunder sheet). There's no point setting up this effect and then producing it via wrongly sited or undersized loudspeakers. To have the impact needed for this sort of effect, you would probably need to use an element of sub bass within the loudspeaker arrangement.

If you were hoping for some help or advice with sound effects, I'm not going to disappoint you altogether, but what I will cover is more to do with the actual 'practical' effects.

The **Wind Machine (2)** is not seen very often these days, in fact never 'seen' at all. It's a behind-the-scenes practical sound effect generator, rarely used now mainly due to the advent and availability of the sound effects CD. The wind machine probably has its origins in a time before the recorded playback of sound effects was even thought possible! It's a practical hand operated device for making the sound of a howling wind. As you will imagine it's an all-timber construction, apart from a piece of canvas. The main feature is something about the shape and size of a bass drum, fitted with a centre spindle and crank handle,

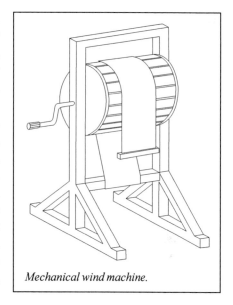

Mechanical wind machine.

mounted in a floor stand. The outer edge of the drum is not solid but a series of wooden lath strips. A piece of scenic canvas about the same width as the drum is fixed to the frame which holds the drum in place and passed over the top of it. This is then fixed onto a wooden batten, which you hold onto at a centre position. The action of the device is somewhat cumbersome, as you turn the handle of the drum while holding onto the canvas and by increasing the speed of rotation while adjusting the angle and tension of the canvas, it produces various sounds that equate to wind, honest – but if you don't build one, you will have to take my word for it.

The humble **Door Slam** is another of those one-off things which you may not use for years, but when you need it, it's the only thing that will do the job. Apart from using it as a live effect that you can use to produce the sound for recording, its main use is as an offstage effect, where someone has made an exit from the main set but the sound of their continued leaving is carried on, off stage. The door slam is a small, simple wooden box, and its size and construction not important. It's the sound of the lock, handle being turned, and the door shutting or slamming that are important. You could also include a door knocker or bell, or of course you could just record the effect and action a sound cue with more modern equipment.

The **Gun Shot.** Yes, of course you can use a blank firing pistol, but these days the availability of such things is rare and often difficult to organise, and for specific on-stage use you will probably need to go to a professional film and theatre armourer. However, if all you need is the sound of a gun shot off stage, or maybe something to record and edit, you could try the Timber gunshot. Take two pieces of timber 75 x 25mm (3 x 1") about 500mm long, fix the two together with a hinge, so that the flat surfaces come together, fit two handles on the outer flat surfaces and there you have it. Just make sure that when you slap it together, you have your fingers and thumbs out of harms way!

The **Rain Machine** is another sound-type effect. Simply described, if you put two tea trays together, one on top of the other, and fill the cavity between them with a good handful of dried split peas and remember to seal the edges to keep the whole lot together, the sound that comes from it when you tilt it gently backwards and forwards produces the sound of rain. You would probably use it in conjunction with a strategically placed microphone and a little backstage amplification. Just like the practical wind machine, it's a little out of date now and the pre-recorded sound effect makes life so much easier.

6 CONCLUSIONS

My guess is that one of the things that may have come as a bit of a surprise to you with almost all of these special effects, is my continual comments about using them in multiples where you probably thought that just one moving cloud effect or gobo image would have done the trick. Of course, just one such effect may be all you need in your application. If so that's great, but just pause to consider what the effect in question looked like, when you saw it in another production and consider the likely quantity of equipment used to create it. If you have never seen the effect elsewhere, just be aware of my comments about the multiple use unless you are working in a relatively small space.

I'll make a wager that when you picked up this book the last thing in your mind was the prospect of making a risk assessment for the use of bubbles in your production. Sadly this seemingly ridiculous situation is sending us all into a self perpetuating downward spiral to nowhere in particular, except to stop, or at least question, things which previously we would have given little or no thought to.

Some would say that we are adopting an attitude from other parts of the world in resorting to law at the first opportunity, and that suing people or avoiding actions that could cause litigation is becoming a national sport.

Some would argue that sometimes people need protection even from themselves, and that our health and safety legislation is there to help us stay safe.

In the real world, the truth is somewhere between these two statements, but since the legislation is in place, like it or loath it, we've all got to work with it.

Leaving all the many unanswered questions relating to heath and safety to one side, I think I'm just about done with special effects. I hope I haven't missed out your favourite, or put you off what you had previously considered simple. Many of you may take the view that almost all of the things you do in mounting a theatrical presentation come under the heading of special effects. After all, you don't see things like performance lighting and sound systems in your everyday activities, much less get involved in setting them up and operating them. So by that very fact, they are all indeed 'special effects'.

I suppose those of us who work within the industry tend to get really quite blasé about it all, and unless they become even more 'special', we tend to take them for granted. I hope you follow the distinction.

I trust you have found the information in this book helpful, even the minefield that is heath and safety. Please remember my intention is just to provide some *'Basic'* information and where special effects are concerned there are sometimes other ways of creating the effect. Have fun with it all, and stay safe.

GLOSSARY

This list is by no means comprehensive. It is intended only to give a quick reference to those names and phrases which often cause most confusion to the beginner.

ABTT Code of Practice
Association of British Theatre Technicians booklet detailing accepted codes of practise for the use of theatrical pyrotechnics (www.abtt.org.uk).

Angled Flash Pod
From the LeMaitre range, the angled box permits certain cartridge effects to be fired at an adjustable angle. See page 24 for details.

Animation Disc
Used in association with a motor drive, fitted to the front of a profile lantern, the animation disc provides a degree of movement where a Gobo is used. Most effective where used in multiples.

BS 7114, 1989
A British Standards Document, detailing four categories of Fireworks.

Black Light
see UV

Bomb Tank
Metal tank with mesh lid, the modern version having internal divisions or sections, used for firing theatrical maroons.

Breakaway
Glass, bottle or simulated pane of glass, made of a clear or coloured resin, used to create the safe breakage of glass for stage effects.

British Pyrotechnists Association
Booklet detailing accepted codes of practise for the use of pyrotechnics (www.bpa-fmg.org.uk).

Bubbles/Bubble Machine
Use of bubbles in stage effects. See page 64.

Coloured Flash
From the LeMaitre range, an instant coloured flash effect cartridge, with white smoke output.

Confetti Cannon
From the LeMaitre range, a small metal container, to be loaded with confetti or other light weight product, using a maroon to detonate the explosive effect. See page 27.

COSHH	*Control Of Substances Hazardous to Health.* Each place of work should have a COSHH register. See page 21.
Detonator	From the LeMaitre range, a two or six channel device, with reporting, selection, key security and firing features, designed for use with LeMaitre products.
Door Slam	Practical off-stage effect. See page 67.
Dry Ice	Solid CO_2 immersed in water gives off a low lying white vapour.
Falling Snow Machine	An effect machine, suspended above the stage, which discharges a pre-loaded polystyrene or paper snow.
Flash Cartridge	From the LeMaitre range, a pre-loaded cartridge, giving a flash effect, with low volume report.
Flash Box	From the LeMaitre range, used in conjunction with the detonator, the Flash Box is the firing base for many pre loaded cartridge effects.
Flicker Stick	A practical effect, a way of simulating flickering flames.
Flicker Candle	A battery operated electric candle.
Gauze Transformation	A transformation effect, using a gauze cloth or panel and lighting. See page 56.
Gobos	A metal or glass disc containing a pattern or picture, used within a profile lantern, thus projecting the image.
Gun Shot	A practical effect, a means of simulating a gun shot without a firearm.
Glass Gobo	Made in glass, this form of Gobo permits the use of colour within the Gobo and also makes possible more delicate almost photographic end results, but at a high price.
Health & Safety Work Act	The Health and Safety at Work Act 1974. This legislation at being titled as an Act is thus a part of British Law.
Haze Machine	A type of smoke machine, with a constant low yield output, used to make the atmosphere haze filled, usually to accentuate lighting effects.

Jumper (maroon)	A short cable providing connection for a theatrical maroon, when fired by a LeMaitre detonator.
Low Smoke Effect	A high power smoke machine plus chiller unit, which causes the smoke to lie on the floor, providing an alternative to the Dry Ice effect.
Magnesium Flash Powder	The main constituent of the explosive charge within many pyrotechnic effects.
Material Safety Data Sheet	Information supplied by a manufacturer, giving details of the product or substance.
Microdet	From the LeMaitre range, a small low report maroon or detonator.
Mirror Ball	A moving (rotating) effect, used with lighting. See page 65.
Moving Head Lantern	A profile or Fresnel lantern, mounted in a motorised yoke.
Moving Projected Image	Using a dedicated projector, a moving effect disc produces a slow moving image.
Practical Flame Effect	A practical effect, using a low power fan, a piece of silk cloth and low power lights, to simulate a flame effect.
Pyrotechnics	The generic family of explosive stage effects.
Rain Effect	A practical sound effect. See page 68.
Risk Assessment	A written statement, identifying risks and operational procedures.
Smoke Detectors	Found in most domestic, commercial and public buildings, smoke detectors will be activated by pyrotechnics and smoke machines.
Smoke Machine	A device for generating large quantities of white smoke.
Smoke Logging	Simply too much smoke within a room or venue.
Snow Bag	A practical effect; a hand operated means of dropping polystyrene or paper snow, from above the stage.

Snow Aerosol	A small hand held aerosol, for the application of small local amounts of simulated snow.
Sound Effects	Any pre-recorded or live sound, used for effect purposes, e.g. thunder.
Stage Trap	A mechanism built in to older theatre stages. See page 51.
Star Cloth	A cloth, normally black, fitted with very small light sources. See page 64.
Strobes	A specific type of lantern using a lamp filament that lights and extinguishes at a very rapid rate, producing a stroboscopic lighting effect. See page 61.
Thunder Sheet	A practical effect, used off stage, to simulate thunder. See page 66.
Tubular Ripple Machine	A lighting effect lantern, producing a rippling water effect. See page 47.
UV (ultraviolet)	A UV lamp or tube, in which the light output and concentrated ultraviolet, used in a blacked out state and in conjunction with UV paints, for various effects.
Up Down Sea Wave	One of the moving effect range. See page 44.
Wind Machine (1)	An electric fan (sizes vary) with speed controls for a real breeze or wind on stage.
Wind Machine (2)	A practical hand-operated sound effect. See page 67.

ENTERTAINMENT TECHNOLOGY PRESS

FREE SUBSCRIPTION SERVICE

Keeping Up To Date with

Basics – A Beginner's Guide to Special Effects

Entertainment Technology titles are continually up-dated, and all major changes and additions are listed in date order in the relevant dedicated area of the publisher's website. Simply go to the front page of www.etnow.com and click on the BOOKS button. From there you can locate the title and be connected through to the latest information and services related to the publication.

The author of the title welcomes comments and suggestions about the book and can be contacted by email at: basics@etnow.com

Titles Published by Entertainment Technology Press

ABC of Theatre Jargon *Francis Reid* **£9.95** ISBN 1904031099
This glossary of theatrical terminology explains the common words and phrases that are used in normal conversation between actors, directors, designers, technicians and managers.

Aluminium Structures in the Entertainment Industry *Peter Hind* **£24.95**
ISBN 1904031064
Aluminium Structures in the Entertainment Industry aims to educate the reader in all aspects of the design and safe usage of temporary and permanent aluminium structures specific to the entertainment industry – such as roof structures, PA towers, temporary staging, etc.

AutoCAD – A Handbook for Theatre Users *David Ripley* **£24.95** ISBN 1904031315
From 'Setting Up' to 'Drawing in Three Dimensions' via 'Drawings Within Drawings', this compact and fully illustrated guide to AutoCAD covers everything from the basics to full colour rendering and remote plotting.

Basics - A Beginner's Guide to Special Effects *Peter Coleman* **£9.95** ISBN 1904031331
This title introduces newcomers to the world of special effects. It describes all types of special effects including pyrotechnic, smoke and lighting effects, projections, noise machines, etc. It places emphasis on the safe storage, handling and use of pyrotechnics.

Basics - A Beginner's Guide to Stage Lighting *Peter Coleman* **£9.95** ISBN 190403120X
This title does what it says: it introduces newcomers to the world of stage lighting. It will not teach the reader the art of lighting design, but will teach beginners much about the 'nuts and bolts' of stage lighting.

Basics - A Beginner's Guide to Stage Sound *Peter Coleman* **£9.95** ISBN 1904031277
This title does what it says: it introduces newcomers to the world of stage sound. It will not teach the reader the art of sound design, but will teach beginners much about the background to sound reproduction in a theatrical environment.

A Comparative Study of Crowd Behaviour at Two Major Music Events
Chris Kemp, Iain Hill, Mick Upton **£7.95** ISBN 1904031099
A compilation of the findings of reports made at two major live music concerts, and in particular crowd behaviour, which is followed from ingress to egress.

Electrical Safety for Live Events *Marco van Beek* **£16.95** ISBN 1904031285
This title covers electrical safety regulations and good pracitise pertinent to the entertainment industries and includes some basic electrical theory as well as clarifying the "do's and don't's" of working with electricity.

The Exeter Theatre Fire *David Anderson* **£24.95** ISBN 1904031137
This title is a fascinating insight into the events that led up to the disaster at the Theatre Royal, Exeter, on the night of September 5th 1887. The book details what went wrong, and the lessons that were learned from the event.

Fading Light - A Year in Retirement *Francis Reid* **£14.95** ISBN 1904031358
Francis Reid, the lighting industry's favourite author, describes a full year in retirement. "Old age is much more fun than I expected," he says. Fading Light describes visits and experiences to the author's favourite theatres and opera houses, places of relaxation and re-visits to scholarly intitutions.

Focus on Lighting Technology *Richard Cadena* **£17.95** ISBN 1904031145
This concise work unravels the mechanics behind modern performance lighting and appeals to designers and technicians alike. Packed with clear, easy-to-read diagrams, the book provides excellent explanations behind the technology of performance lighting.

Health and Safety Aspects in the Live Music Industry *Chris Kemp, Iain Hill* **£30.00** ISBN 1904031226
This title includes chapters on various safety aspects of live event production and is written by specialists in their particular areas of expertise.

Health and Safety Management in the Live Music and Events Industry *Chris Hannam* **£25.95** ISBN 1904031307
This title covers the health and safety regulations and their application regarding all aspects of staging live entertainment events, and is an invaluable manual for production managers and event organisers.

Hearing the Light *Francis Reid* **£24.95** ISBN 1904031188
This highly enjoyable memoir delves deeply into the theatricality of the industry. The author's almost fanatical interest in opera, his formative period as lighting designer at Glyndebourne and his experiences as a theatre administrator, writer and teacher make for a broad and unique background.

An Introduction to Rigging in the Entertainment Industry *Chris Higgs* **£24.95** ISBN 1904031129
This book is a practical guide to rigging techniques and practices and also thoroughly covers safety issues and discusses the implications of working within recommended guidelines and regulations.

Let There be Light - Entertainment Lighting Software Pioneers in Interview *Robert Bell* **£32.00** ISBN 1904031242
Robert Bell interviews a distinguished group of software engineers working on entertainment lighting ideas and products.

Lighting for Roméo and Juliette *John Offord* **£26.95** ISBN 1904031161
John Offord describes the making of the Vienna State Opera production from the lighting designer's viewpoint – from the point where director Jürgen Flimm made his decision not to use scenery or sets and simply employ the expertise of Patrick Woodroffe.

Lighting Systems for TV Studios *Nick Mobsby* **£35.00** ISBN 1904031005
Lighting Systems for TV Studios is the first book written specifically on the subject and is now the 'standard' resource work for the sector as it covers all elements of system design – rigging, ventilation and electrical as well as the more obvious controls, dimmers and luminaires.

Lighting Techniques for Theatre-in-the-Round *Jackie Staines* **£24.95** ISBN 1904031013
Lighting Techniques for Theatre-in-the-Round is a unique reference source for those working on lighting design for theatre-in-the-round for the first time. It is the first title to be published specifically on the subject, it also provides some anecdotes and ideas for more challenging shows, and attempts to blow away some of the myths surrounding lighting in this format.

Lighting the Stage *Francis Reid* **£14.95** ISBN 1904031080
Lighting the Stage discusses the human relationships involved in lighting design – both between people, and between these people and technology. The book is written from a highly personal viewpoint and its 'thinking aloud' approach is one that Francis Reid has used in his writings over the past 30 years.

Model National Standard Conditions *ABTT/DSA/LGLA* **£20.00** ISBN 1904031110
These *Model National Standard Conditions* covers operational matters and complement *The Technical Standards for Places of Entertainment*, which describes the physical requirements for building and maintaining entertainment premises.

Pages From Stages *Anthony Field* **£17.95** ISBN 1904031269
Anthony Field explores the changing style of theatres including interior design, exterior design, ticket and seat prices, and levels of service, while questioning whether the theatre still exists as a place of entertainment for regular theatre-goers.

Practical DMX *Nick Mobsby* **£14.95** ISBN 19040313668
In this highly topical and important title, the author discusses DMX Networks and Installations and the equipment involved. Analogue networks are also covered and there is an introduction to Ethernet networks and cabling systems.

Practical Guide to Health and Safety in the Entertainment Industry
Marco van Beek **£14.95** ISBN 1904031048
This book is designed to provide a practical approach to Health and Safety within the Live Entertainment and Event industry. It gives industry-pertinent examples, and seeks to break down the myths surrounding Health and Safety.

Production Management *Joe Aveline* **£17.95** ISBN 1904031102
Joe Aveline's book is an in-depth guide to the role of the Production Manager, and includes real-life practical examples and 'Aveline's Fables' – anecdotes of his experiences with real messages behind them.

Rigging for Entertainment: Regulations and Practice *Chris Higgs* **£19.95**
ISBN 1904031218
Continuing where he left off with his highly successful *An Introduction to Rigging in the Entertainment Industry*, Chris Higgs' second title covers the regulations and use of equipment in greater detail.

Rock Solid Ethernet *Wayne Howell* **£24.95** ISBN 1904031293
Although aimed specifically at specifiers, installers and users of entertainment industry systems, this book will give the reader a thorough grounding in all aspects of computer networks, whatever industry they may work in. The inclusion of historical and technical 'sidebars' make for an enjoyable as well as informative read.

Sixty Years of Light Work *Fred Bentham* **£26.95** ISBN 1904031072
This title is an autobiography of one of the great names behind the development of modern stage lighting equipment and techniques.

Sound for the Stage *Patrick Finelli* **£24.95** ISBN 1904031153
Patrick Finelli's thorough manual covering all aspects of live and recorded sound for performance is a complete training course for anyone interested in working in the field of stage sound, and is a must for any student of sound.

Stage Lighting for Theatre Designers *Nigel Morgan* **£17.95** ISBN 1904031196
This is an updated second edition of Nigel Morgan's popular book for students of theatre design – outlining all the techniques of stage lighting design.

Technical Marketing Techniques *David Brooks, Andy Collier, Steve Norman* **£24.95** ISBN 190403103X
Technical Marketing is a novel concept, recently defined and elaborated by the authors of this book, with business-to-business companies competing in fast developing technical product sectors.

Technical Standards for Places of Entertainment *ABTT/DSA* **£30.00** ISBN 1904031056
Technical Standards for Places of Entertainment details the necessary physical standards required for entertainment venues.

Theatre Engineering and Stage Machinery *Toshiro Ogawa* **£30.00** ISBN 1904031021
Theatre Engineering and Stage Machinery is a unique reference work covering every aspect of theatrical machinery and stage technology in global terms, and across the complete historical spectrum.

Theatre Lighting in the Age of Gas *Terence Rees* **£24.95** ISBN 190403117X
Entertainment Technology Press has republished this valuable historic work previously produced by the Society for Theatre Research in 1978. *Theatre Lighting in the Age of Gas* investigates the technological and artistic achievements of theatre lighting engineers from the 1700s to the late Victorian period.

Walt Disney Concert Hall *Patricia MacKay & Richard Pilbrow* **£28.95** ISBN 1904031234
Spanning the 16-year history of the design and construction of the Walt Disney Concert Hall, this book provides a fresh and detailed behind the scenes story of the design and technology from a variety of viewpoints. This is the first book to reveal the "process" of the design of a concert hall.

Yesterday's Lights – A Revolution Reported *Francis Reid* **£26.95** ISBN 1904031323
Set to help new generations to be aware of where the art and science of theatre lighting is coming from – and stimulate a nostalgia trip for those who lived through the period, Francis Reid's latest book has over 350 pages dedicated to the task, covering the 'revolution' from the fifties through to the present day. Although this is a highly personal account of the development of lighting design and technology and he admits that there are 'gaps', you'd be hard put to find anything of significance missing.

Go to www.etbooks.co.uk for full details of above titles and secure online ordering facilities.